LANIGAN
IN THE MORNING

LANIGAN
IN THE MORNING
— MY LIFE IN RADIO —
JOHN LANIGAN

with Peter Jedick
and Mike Olszewski

GRAY & COMPANY, PUBLISHERS
CLEVELAND

Gray & Company, Publishers
www.grayco.com

ISBN: 978-1-938441-93-6
Printed in the U.S.A.

1

Dedicated to Jack Thayer,
without whom none of this
would have ever happened.
And also my wife, Sandy.

Contents

Preface

WHEN I STARTED WRITING this memoir, I was doing a radio show on WTAM-AM with Mike Trivisonno called *The Spew*—an hour-long morning show in which Triv and I debate the hot topics of the day. One day our program director passed along a letter he had received from one of our listeners. When he gave it to me he said, "You've got to read this, John." I did, and it was an amazing letter.

The two-page letter was from a woman, just an ordinary, every-day person sitting out there listening to our show. She had listed each of the topics we'd talked about recently and added her own view. It wasn't negative and it wasn't positive. It was just her thoughts about the show—a balanced criticism of issues she saw as important, like her view of the presidential elections that were going on at the time.

For example, she asked, "Do you notice how Hillary always has her husband or her daughter along with her and you don't see any of the rest of them with their families?" It was just things that she had thought of while she listened. She had quite a story herself. She was on welfare, getting food stamps, didn't have any money, and was having a hard time getting through life. Her description about what it was like to go through life like that was enough to make you cry.

At the end of the letter she said, "Please write a book. You've had such an interesting life and met so many people, and I enjoy it when you talk about your travels. You might think that people don't want to read about you, but you're wrong. I think it would just be wonderful."

Then she added, "Please ask Triv to stop saying 'Okay' after everything. It's annoying."

What she had to say really caught me off guard. (Well, not the part about Triv.) At the time I was considering writing this memoir, so I couldn't help but think as I read it, *if I do write one, you're going to get the first copy.*

As you can see, I did write a book (with help from a couple of friends). And she's getting the first copy.

Introduction

I WAS WALKING THROUGH CLEVELAND Hopkins Airport with my son Jad, his wife, and my grandkids when seven-year-old Natalie let out a scream. "Grandpa, that's us!" she yelled, looking at the nearby *Plain Dealer* newspaper box. There was a front-page photo of the two of us sitting in my glass radio booth. It had been taken the day before, my last day behind the microphone at WMJI-FM. Of course, I had to run over and buy a few copies of the paper. And that's when it finally sank in. On March 31, 2014, after almost fifty years as a morning radio talk show host, it was over. No more waking up at four in the morning for our 5:30 start time. No more "Knuckleheads in the News." No more traffic updates.

My last two weeks on the air were pretty hectic. In fact, it was overwhelming. A lot of old friends in and out of the business had stopped by or called in to wish me farewell. I had wanted to slip out quietly at the end of the calendar year, but Keith Abrams, my program director, convinced me to stick around and help promote WMJI's annual "Moondog Coronation" concert, a tribute to the old-time rock and rollers who symbolized our station's format.

I really got an idea of how radio affected people. Tommy James was one of the acts at a Moondog show, and he had had a lot of big radio hits. I went backstage to say hello, and we really hit it off. We started talking about radio jingles, and it turns out we were both fans of WLS-AM in Chicago. People walking past the dressing room could hear us belting out WLS jingles.

Sly and the Family Stone was one of the featured groups at that show, though of course the original Sly was not with them. His replacement was a singer from Akron who remembered watching my *Prize Movie* television show when he was a kid. That's going way back. The more everyone kept remembering the past, the older I began to feel. It was time to move on, and I knew it.

On my last day at the radio station they had a cake for me. I thanked everyone for their kindness, but I just wanted to go home. They gave me my microphone, and I threw it into a box of other souvenirs. As my son Jad helped me carry my souvenirs out to my car, I heard someone say, "Lanigan has left the building."

Chapter One

The Early Years

THERE'S SOMETHING ABOUT NEBRASKA. Maybe it's in the water. A lot of entertainers came out Nebraska. Johnny Carson, Dick Cavett, Henry Fonda, Marlon Brando. The list goes on and on. Oh, one more. I'm from Ogallala, Nebraska. I wasn't born there. That happened in San Diego, where my dad was stationed at a military base. He decided to relocate to Nebraska to help my grandfather with his hardware business. My grandfather was traveling around the state with a partner named Cabela. That's right, the same guy whose stores are now all over the country. But back then he was on the road, and my grandfather wanted to stay in one location. My family settled in Ogallala and that's where I eventually discovered this thing called radio.

But radio is not where I thought I would end up.

Football isn't a sport in Nebraska. It's a way of life. It's almost a religion! Just about every kid wants to be a Cornhusker, and I was no different. In high school the football heroes got the girls, and that was plenty of incentive for me. Here's the problem, though: One day I hurt myself running out onto the field. Seriously! I was an end with the Ogallala Indians, and we were playing an away game against the team from Alliance. As the team was running out of the locker room and up a concrete ramp, my cleat got caught on something and *wham!* I went down hard on my elbow, and I mean really hard. The other guys kept running past me, telling me to get up, but I knew I had to head the other way. I stumbled over to the coach and said, "I . . . I think I broke my arm!" He gave me a weird look. "What? You didn't even make it to the *field!*" Sorry, coach. Afraid not. A doctor looked me over, and it was pretty serious—a dislocated elbow. And that pretty much brought an end to my football career. I had a feeling that athletics weren't my strong suit.

Now what?

There weren't many options for things to do after school in Ogallala. I could have joined the marching band, but I didn't play an instrument, so my opportunities there were limited. Also, that would have put me right back on the football field—and I could take a hint. There was always Future Farmers of America, which is a fine organization but not exactly a magnet for the opposite sex.

One other option caught my attention. A kid in my school had an afternoon gig at KOGA, a little radio station at 930 on the AM dial. It was the only station in town. (There were no FMs, and even if there had been, no one had a tuner that could receive them.) There were about five thousand people in town, but KOGA had a bigger audience than that. In fact, the air signal covered most of western Nebraska. Word got around that this guy, who was a couple of classes ahead of me, would soon be moving on, so a position might be opening up. It seemed to make a lot more sense to be heard on the air than be seen getting pounded on the field. *Let's see where this goes,* I thought. I found myself knocking on the door at KOGA.

Big surprise: They hired me!

This was a great time to be in radio. It was the late 1950s, the

I was still in high school when I started spinning records at KOGA radio in Ogallala, Nebraska, the only station in town. Circa 1958.

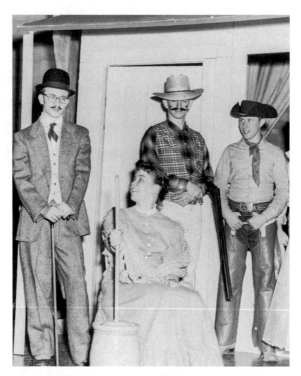

I caught the acting bug playing Ali Hakim in our high
school production of *Oklahoma* in Ogallala, Nebraska.
That's me on the far left. Circa 1958.

first era of rock and roll, and disc jockeys got to pick what they
played. Truth be told, I also bought many of the records I played
with money I earned at the hardware store.

Oh yeah, I should explain that. I hung out at a record store next
to my dad's store, and I would check out the new releases. But
then I got a little carried away and started slipping them into my
portfolio. Okay, if you want put it that way, I was stealing them,
but here's why. I had set up a rehearsal studio at my house. I'd
sit in my basement and write out a playlist. Then I'd put the 45s
on the spindle of an old record player and introduce them like

I was on the big radio stations coming out of Oklahoma City or Chicago.

This was a pretty good way to get records—until I got caught red-handed. Needless to say, the proprietor wasn't happy. He pulled me through the door at my dad's store and told my dad, "Your son stole these records!" This put my dad in an awkward position, and I knew I was in it up to my neck. Dad laid down the law. "You're going to repay him for all those records one way or the other," he said, and that's just what I did. I never stole anything again after that.

It was a wake-up call.

I had a great job at a great time for the industry. DJs talked about the artists, and their personalities were important parts of that whole entertainment package. I knew this was where I belonged. I didn't want to lose it. I fell in love with that job—one that would treat me very well for close to fifty years. I never forgot that incident.

Ogallala, Nebraska, was typical small-town America, and it was a hoot! Radio was the life for me. It was a fun job for a young guy. I had a chance to do stuff at the schools, like run sock hops. Back at the studio, I got to play records and do newscasts and try to pronounce words that I didn't know. Sometimes I got them right. One time I used the words "Cesarean section" on a newscast, but pronounced it, "serisian." My mom was one of my listeners (and my biggest fan), and when I got home she corrected me. Not only couldn't I pronounce it, I didn't even know what it meant. She explained the procedure and how to say it correctly. I went through a lot of stuff like that, trying to learn new words, but I had a good coach.

Working fires was another stumbling block. My station was the voice of Ogallala, and if there was a fire in town everyone tuned in to hear the latest. The fire reports were all sponsored by the L.J.

Wittenburg Insurance Company, which seemed to make sense because if your house burned down you'd better have coverage. I was always supposed to end the newscast by saying, "Please do not follow the fire truck, as it is against the law." I don't know why, but for some reason I would always get it wrong and say, "Please do not fire the follow truck." Everyone heard it, and I took plenty of grief until I eventually got it right.

When you start out in radio, you wear a lot of different hats and work a lot of hours. For me, it was after school and on weekends. It doesn't seem like work, though, if you're having fun. After a while, folks knew who I was, and I knew this was the job for me.

When the time came for me to graduate from high school and pick a college, I broke the news to my mom that I wanted a career in radio instead. She had some news for me, too.

"That's nice," she said. "I know you're having a good time, but you need a real job, something you can do for a living. What if you lose your voice?"

Lose my voice? Who loses their voice? I could see if you were a baseball pitcher and broke your arm or your leg, but how many people ever really lose their voice? I knew she was just trying to discourage me, but I didn't want to disappoint her, so I enrolled at the University of Nebraska.

I was hooked on media, though. At the university, I did some camera work for the campus TV station, worked at the college radio station, and listened to the Top 40 station in Lincoln.

Then a car accident sent me back home, where my life took a dramatic turn.

My father took me aside and said he didn't have enough money to send both me and my younger brother, Pat, to college. I faced facts. Pat was a lot smarter than me. So I told my dad that was fine, and I'd rather do radio anyway. College just didn't appeal to me.

Instead, I took a course in radio broadcasting. I seemed to

One of my favorite gigs in high school was acting as emcee and spinning records at the VFW high school dances in Ogallala, Nebraska. That's me with my back to the camera. Circa 1958.

know more about the industry than my professor, though, thanks to my high school gig. He had a college degree but no real work experience. He would come visit me at the college radio station and ask me questions about what I was doing. Who was teaching whom?

There was a radio station in Scottsbluff, Nebraska, KEYR-AM, "The Key." I was able to land a job there and go to the junior college at night. The station was owned by Terry Carpenter, the senior senator from Nebraska, but it was still a small operation. He put me in morning drive until 9 a.m., and I programmed the station. This is my first job out of Ogallala! I picked out the station's play list, and they paid me a few hundred bucks a week to boot. Life was good! I rented an apartment next door to the station, and my morning commute was a run across the lawn. Ogallala was in the rear-view mirror.

I soon came to realize that if I wanted this to continue, I had to be different. That's when I decided to start doing comedy bits in the show. I wanted to be like my radio idol, Dick Biondi, out of WLS in Chicago. He called himself the "Wild I-tralian" because he had an Italian accent. Biondi even had a hit record, a novelty song called "On Top of a Pizza," to the tune of "On Top of Old Smoky." I just thought Dick Biondi was the best, and how great it would be to be like him. He played all the records, made all the funny comments. This guy was a disc jockey!

I don't want to get too far ahead of myself, but this is a good place for my Dick Biondi story. I got to meet him a few years ago when I was introducing my friend, John Gorman, into one of the broadcast halls of fame. As I started my introduction, I noticed Biondi sitting in the crowd. I was thrilled. I told the crowd, "Before I go any farther, I have to go see Dick Biondi, who is also being inducted." I ran down to where he was sitting, shook his hand, and said, "I got my start in the business listening to you. WLS was like my friend. I'm glad you're here because you are something else." Oh yeah—Gorman! I went back to the podium and finished the introduction. It was an emotional moment for me. I never got to meet up with Dick Biondi again, so I'm glad that I jumped at that opportunity.

Dick Biondi was big-time radio, and that's what I wanted to be. Scottsbluff was a stepping stone. It wasn't long before I ended up taking a bigger step, to Denver, though in a really strange way.

I had a girlfriend at the University of Colorado and would visit her on the weekends. There was a jock named Perry Allen at KTLN out of Denver who was pretty funny. I wanted to add comedy to my gig, so I would write down his jokes and take them back with me to Scottsbluff. Hey, I was young. Stealing jokes wasn't nearly as bad as stealing records when I was a kid. I eventually heard that Allen was moving his show to KRLA in Los Angeles. So I sent in a tape to KTLN, thinking there was no way I would ever get the job. This is where it gets weird.

It turned out that Perry Allen was from Scottsbluff, Nebraska! Not only that, his wife would go back to his home from time to time to visit his parents, and when she was there she would listen to my radio show. So when the time came to decide on Allen's successor, she told the folks in charge they should give the guy in Scottsbluff a listen.

"He's pretty good," she told them. What she didn't know was that I was pretty good because I was using her husband's jokes. Allen went to the program director, Joe Finan, and told him about me. Finan said he already had a tape from me, and they gave it a listen and then offered me the job. Is that crazy or what?

Here's something else that's just as nutty. Years later, I met Perry Allen in Los Angeles. He told me about his wife recommending me, and I said that she liked me because I was using his jokes. He thought that was funny. And maybe he was impressed with my honesty, because a few years after that he even gave me the index cards that he kept his jokes on. He was retiring and didn't need them anymore. A great guy.

So I ended up going from the minors to the big leagues. Could that happen the same way today? Not likely. Nowadays, there just aren't the same opportunities for young people. The best part of starting out in high school was that it had let me be bad. I learned from the rookie mistakes, and also how to talk over the fronts and backs of the songs. Today they would get rid of someone like me. They want you to be good right away. It's hard to find somewhere to go where you can make a lot of mistakes. They want someone who is already a pro. If you strike out, there's someone else warming up in the on-deck circle.

I didn't make any money. But it was somewhere to learn. There were no broadcast schools back then, and Top 40 radio was pretty new. They were looking for people to work weekends and holidays, so I'd do whatever they wanted. Even in Denver, I'd work the holidays. Got to say, it was worth it!

Chapter Two

The Denver Years

KTLN IN DENVER WAS a place to learn, but you had to learn quickly. Years later, as I was sifting through the dusty memories from that time, I realized there was an elephant in the room that I should discuss.

My years in Denver were pretty crazy, from the day I started to the last time I signed off, and they all revolved around my boss. Joe Finan was the man in charge, and he had a colorful past—in Cleveland, at WERE. It involved the payola scandal back in the 1950s.

Here's the way it worked back then: Record companies and managers would pay disc jockeys in cash or "favors." The mob had its fingers in jukeboxes and record companies and it needed hits to keep the revenue flowing. The artists didn't really make anything, but if they wanted a career, they had to play ball with some pretty unsavory characters. When they weren't in the studio they were on the road promoting their records, all for pennies. Meanwhile, the guys at the record labels had limos, houses in the Hamptons and the best of everything. Some of them even put themselves down as the co-writers of hit songs to get the publishing rights.

The DJs could get a piece of that if they cooperated and played certain records in heavy rotation. Oh, and those favors I mentioned? Cars, booze, hookers—you name it. Just keep playing those records. It was standard operating procedure back then, and it wasn't illegal. The jocks who got busted hadn't claimed the gifts on their tax forms. That's what was illegal. You don't mess with the IRS. After all, they had taken down Al Capone—and bunch of guys playing records were like fish in a barrel.

Years later there was speculation that Alan Freed was targeted because he was playing black music for white audiences and wouldn't allow segregated audiences. They arrested him in Boston for that. Oh, and Joe Finan. He was one of the poster boys for payola, but to his credit, he took the rap for a lot of other guys and didn't rat out anyone else, even though it was a pretty common practice back then. That's how he ended up at KTLN-FM in Denver. He hired me in the early '60s when I was barely out of high school. Finan also gave me an education I couldn't get in college.

I was working the night shift and the studio was at the street level overlooking the parking lot on the side of the building. It was right on Colfax Street, which was the main roadway in Denver. I took calls during my show, and one night a caller said, "Hi. You see that window in front of you right there?" Yeah. "I'm going to shoot you through it!" *Click!* What the hell do I do now!?

Some other folks were at the station, and we called the cops. Thankfully, there was no sign of anybody outside. But there wasn't a day that I came into work after that when I didn't look out that window and think, "I wonder if somebody's going to shoot me through that window today."

Oh, and in Denver my all-night news guy later made a name for himself at CBS: Harry Smith! Now, back to Finan.

That window gave me a beautiful view of downtown Denver

and, as it turned out, a lot more. One night I looked out to see two guys fighting, and they meant business—really banging on each other. And I was watching it like it was a prizefight on TV. Then I realized it was my crazy boss, Joe Finan, and Al Julius, the news director. I learned later that they had started fighting in the studio during my show, took it out across Colfax Street and through the front doors of Sid King's Crazy Horse Bar, a notorious strip joint. Someone inside yelled, "Call the police!" That apparently was a call back to reality, because Finan and Julius ran out a back door in separate directions. They both made it home and the cops never caught them or even figured out who they were. The next day they came back to work like nothing had happened.

Finan was a crazy man, and he was certainly in the right business. He also had some weird ideas about my show.

Finan wanted my show to sound like it came from a nightclub. He wanted excitement, with sound effects in the background, while we played comedy records by the Smothers Brothers or Bill Cosby. We'd say, "Live in downtown Denver from 'Club Chamera.'" There was no real Club Chamera; it was a name we made up. We also gave out a phony address and people would try to find a nightclub that didn't exist! We'd play cuts from albums with sound effects and make it seem like the Smothers Brothers were really there. I was also supposed to sound like I was in that club every night, but Finan wasn't convinced. "I'm listening to you, and you don't sound like you're in a night club," he said. I told him it was hard for me because I wasn't old enough to go to a nightclub. I wasn't even 21 years old.

"Look," I told him, "it's hard to sound like you're in a nightclub if you've never been in one. But you've never been out of one. For god's sake, you're always in the clubs." I might have used some discretion before I said that.

One night I was doing my show and the door swang open. It

was Finan, and he'd had a few drinks. He sat down at the mic and told me to get out. "Let me show you how it should sound," he said. I have to admit, he sounded great doing it. Good reason, too. Finan was in the bars all the time and he knew how to make it sound real. I said that I'd go back on and do the best I could to make it work, but I never really could. Let's face it, he had a lot more practice, in and out of the studio.

Finan was a crazy guy who sounded great on the air, and Al Julius was a great newsman. They both stayed at the station for a long time after I left. Finan also gave me a glimpse into my own future.

He used to tell me stories about Cleveland radio, and it sounded like such a great place to work. There was big talent there, and rock and roll was king. That was my introduction to Cleveland, from a guy who had been there for a long time. Finan had even done TV, dressed up as a service station attendant, your "Atlantic Weatherman."

Finan never talked about the payola scandals in Cleveland, at least not to me. From everything I had heard, he had ended up in Denver to avoid any more problems. He took most of the blame, even though plenty of other people had been involved, and I always gave him credit for that. I also know that he hadn't wanted to leave Cleveland. Those were good times, talking to Joe Finan. Until the axe fell.

After about a year and a half, he fired me. He was pretty blunt, too. Called me in and said, "I don't like the sound of it. You're fired." I'm still not really sure why. He used the old line that he had "decided to go in another direction." To be honest, I wasn't that good yet anyway, so I didn't hold a grudge.

A few years later Finan ended up back in Cleveland, and one of the first things he said, jokingly, was, "I'm going to go after that Lanigan. I fired that punk when I was in Denver and I can knock him out of the box again." Didn't happen. After a few years at WHK, he ended up working in Akron until he died.

After being fired in Denver I ended up in Colorado Springs, where I did the morning show at KVOR. Thanks to some friends back in Denver, I was also able to go back and do the all-night show at KIMN, so I was driving back and forth between Colorado Springs and Denver every day. It worked out pretty well until one day I got a call from Nelson Doubleday, Jr., the guy who owned the company. "We're going to move you," he said. *Uh, oh. Where to this time?* "I'm sending you to Albuquerque, New Mexico. We have a great station there; you'll love it." I wasn't sold.

"What is that? Sand and Mexicans?" I asked. I really didn't want to go there but I needed the gig and found out there is so much more than sand and Mexicans in New Mexico.

My general manager was Johnny Siquerious. He was Mexican, and probably the best boss I ever had. He was the program director, and a kind and thoughtful person who took me aside and taught me things. That includes humility.

Coming out of Denver, I went to Albuquerque with this big opinion of myself. One day I was giving some of the staff there a hard time. John took me aside. He said, "Come on. Lighten up a little bit. These guys have been here for quite a while. Maybe they haven't been where you have, but you know what? They are trying really hard." Siquerious just had this friendly, reassuring way and he sure knew how to communicate. I listened to everything he said to me, and I learned everything I could. He was a major influence.

I tried to find him in later years, but couldn't. His brother was from Mexico City, where he was a famous artist who painted murals on the walls of the university there. He was just a wonderful human being and I had a great time working for him. Hey John, if you happen to be reading this . . .

In radio your only security is the money you have in the bank, so you're always looking to put away as much as you can for the future. One day I went over to one of the local television stations, trying for a voice-over gig. I talked to the manager and he said, "What we need is a weatherman. Do you have any TV experience?"

He caught me off guard with that one. "I'm sorry. What?"

"A TV weatherman. We're looking for one. Do you have any experience?" I had to say no, but he said, "I'd like to try you out, but I'm not going to put you on because you wear glasses. You'll have to get rid of them and get contacts. I'll pay for the contacts and make you the TV weatherman. Since you're on the radio in the morning, you can have some fun promoting us back and forth."

Sometimes the planets just align the right way! I got the contacts, got the gig and went to work as a weatherman. Just like Finan in Cleveland, but I didn't wear a uniform like I wanted to check your oil and water. With my radio show it was a long day, but I got to work with the top news team in Albuquerque.

Dick Knipfing was the anchor, and he was really well known and respected. A lifer, too. He'd been there for 20 years and was a great guy. Gene Osborn, the sports guy, had come down from Chicago, where he was the voice of the Cubs. And then there was Lanigan, the weather guy, to round it out. So it was the three of us for four years. I had a ball. Not much sleep, but plenty of fun!

The guys were great, but there was a slight problem. We still needed something to talk about, and the weather in Albuquerque was so predictable, it could be recorded a month in advance. There wasn't much change. Maybe a little snow once in a while, since we were at the foot of mountains, but that was about it. I might have been channeling David Letterman's weather gig in Indianapolis at that point, even though I'd never heard of him. I used to wear outrageous neckties that people would send me and we would make fun of them. Once I even cut one of them in two on the air because I didn't like it. People loved the abuse. So I was the crazy weatherman, and I had fun doing it. Plus, I got to be known all over the state, since there were only four channels. Once I was in the Carlsbad Caverns and some guy came up and said, "Hey, aren't you that weatherman, Lanigan? How are you?" *Right now, just like you—underground, dark, and damp.* But enjoying life.

We even opened up a nightclub. It was called The Rectory, like at a church. It was a rock and roll club, and we had a lot of good acts. One night the manager came over to me and said, "You know who's over there? Three Dog Night!" They were one of the hottest acts on the charts at the time, but we didn't bug them to get on stage. Everyone needs a night off now and again. This was some life I was leading. I had the radio show, the TV show and the nightclub.

I was doing pretty well. I had my radio show in the morning and I was doing weather on the ABC-TV affiliate every night. But the only constant in the radio industry is change. One day word came that KOB radio was going to do something to stop me, and they were bringing in a new guy—from Cleveland! *Oh, shit!* I thought. *Cleveland's coming in. I'm dead! He'll kill me now. He'll wipe me out.* I don't even remember the new guy's name now, but he didn't do much in Albuquerque.

It was around 1969 when Doubleday called and said he was moving me to another station. *Hmm . . . what options do I have?* I could have turned it down, but my goal was to get into really big-market radio. Even so, I loved Albuquerque and I still think if I could live anywhere in the world it would be Santa Fe. I hated to leave Albuquerque. The radio was fine. The weather was good and we had a house right on the Rio Grande with horses. Still, it was probably time to move on.

They shipped me back to KHOW, their station in Denver. Hal

Davis was the general manager there and he also did the morning show, using the name Elmer Fox. Now, there's a radio name, but he was a legend. He put me on mid-mornings, but gave up his morning drive show not long after I got there. Guess who got the nod to replace him? I became the morning man on KHOW Denver, the number-one show in the city, and I knew darn well it was up to the new guy to replace a legend and keep up the ratings.

I just decided to have a really good time.

My best friend, Casey Cook, owned a night club called Marvelous Marv's, and I was finally old enough to drink. Marv's was the top nightclub in that part of the country. It was mentioned on national television a lot because everybody who was anybody in the area played there. Whether it was the Eagles visiting their recording studio outside of town or anybody else who came in there, they made it a point to show up at Marv's.

I got to know some of the legends, too. The Drifters played there a lot, and I was the master of ceremonies for all their shows because . . . all right, it was convenient. I was living upstairs in the same building as the nightclub, I'd walk down every night and we'd do a show. I'd introduce all the acts, and I got to work with the Drifters so often they considered me an honorary "blood brother."

A lot of the entertainers and comedians who came through there were later on my show in Cleveland. I remember once when we had comedian Fred Willard, he said, "I know your name. I used to see it on the marquee at Marvelous Marv's. You were the emcee!"

It was a great club and a great time in my life. I'd get up early in the morning, drive to work at the station, do my show and then end up at the club that night. Casey Cook and I spent some quality time together.

Some big-name guests came through KHOW, too. John Denver

When I worked briefly for a radio station in Albuquerque, New Mexico, they sent me to participate in a bull fight in Tijuana, Mexico. As part of the promotion I stood in the middle of the ring and let the bull make a couple passes by me. Luckily, the bull wasn't a very big.

was one of them. I really liked his music, but even more so, I really liked him as a person. He was a fun guy, and as it turned out, a great friend.

I remember playing golf with John and his dad, and I'll admit it, I was a terrible golfer. I was about to tee off when John walked right in front of me. I stopped my swing and I asked him, "What the hell was that all about?"

"That's okay, John," he said, "I was out of your range." You know what? He was probably right!

By that time he had left the Chad Mitchell Trio and was traveling around on his own. He had just returned from Washington, D.C. He always had a standing invitation to be on our show so he just showed up and asked if he could come in. That door was always open. He brought his guitar with him, and we talked a little bit about him being in D.C., what he was working on, and how his music was really starting to get a lot of attention. Then he mentioned, "We wrote this last night and I thought I'd like to try it." *Okay, let's give it a listen.*

The tune had never been played anywhere before and we decided to roll tape. We recorded everything anyway. The song was called "Take Me Home, Country Road." You might remember it as a huge hit, but it had never been heard before that morning. This was a scoop!

"I love it!" I told John. "I think it's great!" We used that recording on our show before a record was actually released. The record soared up the charts, and John Denver thanked me with a gold record—and you can bet that I still have it.

Remember Doug Kershaw? He appeared frequently on *The Merv Griffin Show* and the variety shows. He was part of Rusty and Doug, who had a big hit back then called "Louisiana Man." It had a Cajun sound. Kind of different, but a great hit.

I had a show at the Hilton Hotel on Friday nights and we would have people come in and play. The hotel had a club called Lulu Belle's and on Saturday nights it was known as Lanigan's Living Room. I'd try to get whomever I could to play there. So one night I got John Denver and Doug Kershaw to come over and play together, and it was one of our best nights ever. The line at the Hilton was out the door and around the block.

They played their music for an hour. John did "Country Road,"

I dressed in a bride's outfit for a charity promotion while working at KHOW radio in Denver. And guess what? I won the "Best Dressed as a Woman" contest. Next to me is the station's sports guy, Mike Wolfe.

Doug had "Louisiana Man," and then they played some of their other hits. The crowd ate it up! It was one of the most amazing concerts I ever saw, and it was just an impromptu thing on a nice stage. That was the magic of the Colorado music scene.

There was a lot of action in Denver outside the clubs, too. I was working just as *Lanigan in the Morning*—a solo gig, no partner— but we always had someone in the studio. One of the guests started talking about skydiving, and I thought I'd like to try it.

"Well, then, why don't you?" the guest asked. Sounded like a good idea and he even offered to help. Even so, I didn't want to do it alone.

"I want the rest of the show to do it with me," I said. "Maybe we can make it a fun thing to do."

So five brave folks from the staff got together and learned how to skydive, and it turned into a promotion. We talked on the air about going out to the mountains in Denver and skydiving together and, sure enough, we did it. Okay, we did it with various degrees of success. Truth is, I almost landed on a cow. It was pretty close because I wasn't really good at it, but we all did it and nobody got hurt. Even "Captain Show Biz," the manager who later fired me, joined us. It was a hell of a good promotion. Lots of people showed up down below to watch the jump, and I got a lot of exposure out of it. I liked it so much that later I did it on my own.

Sometimes the promotions were small; others were huge. For one of the smaller ones in Denver, we sponsored a contest where we all dressed up as women. The idea was to see who was the best-looking one on the stage. I was dressed as a bride and won as the best-looking female. Okay, nothing to be terribly proud of, but it was a fun promotion. The judges all had white canes but . . .

For one of our bigger promotions, we raced dog sleds. The Iditarod dog sled race was big news in Alaska, so we figured we could do the same thing in Denver. It was a typical Colorado winter and it gave us an excuse to do something outside. So we took a dog sled team up to a town in the Rocky Mountains. I believe it was Idaho Springs, Colorado. There were about five teams of dog sleds—another radio station and a couple of local politicians got in on the act with us. After we learned how to work with the dogs, we raced from one side of the town to the other. It was great fun. It was just cool standing on the sled with the dogs pulling us.

We had a really big turnout and it was great for the community.

In Denver, I drove a team of dogs as a promotion in Idaho Springs, Colorado.
The sled is on wheels, not skis, because there was no snow.

We were raising money for some charity. When we buckled up
the dogs they started going crazy. We hollered out, "Let's go, let's
go!" and they started barking and woofing, all ready to go. The
dogs were pros, too. They gave a great show. I don't remember
who won but it was just the experience of holding the reins of a
dog sled that I got a real kick out of. Those were the kind of promotions that you could do in those days, but you don't see much
of that anymore.

Denver wasn't all fun and games. It's also where I got divorced
and remarried. When my first wife threw me out, I packed all my
things in my car and parked about a block away from the radio
station at 16th and Broadway. It was cold and snowy, and when
I came out after my shift somebody had broken into the car and

stolen all my clothes. This was a part of the career I hadn't antic-ipated.

So now I had no clothes and nowhere to live. Luckily, a friend reached out.

"I understand you have a problem and need someplace to stay," said Bobby Rifkin, who owned a nightclub called Fridays that was a really hot at the time. "I'm going to help you because you always helped me."

"I didn't help you at all," I responded.

Rifkin disagreed. "Didn't you put the people I asked about on the air for me all the time?"

Yeah, but they were stars. That was no big favor. We had The New Christy Minstrels on because they were The New Christy Minstrels. He had a lot of people coming through like that, so we'd put them on the air.

Rifkin remembered. "You always helped me," he insisted, "so there's a hotel room in your name that you can stay in until you find your own place."

I appreciated Rifkin's help but I didn't want to be indebted to him, so I checked out after a few days. There was a band at the Playboy Club and I knew one of the guys who had a spare bedroom. Well, it wasn't really a bedroom. It was more like a mattress on the floor, but with a sheet and blanket it was good enough. I would roll off the mattress, head to work at the top-rated morning show in town, and eventually I was back on the mattress on the floor. That keeps you humble.

Folks looked out for me and I appreciated it, but I also had to be independent. It wasn't long before I got my own place, at Brooks Towers, one of the better apartment complexes in down-town Denver. It was easy to find. The club I worked at, Marvelous Marv's, was just downstairs, so I took an elevator down at night to do my emcee gig and then rode it back up to my place until morning. The radio station was only a few blocks away, so things were settling into place. There were even better changes on the way.

That's when I met my wife, Sandra. The afternoon guy at KHOW, Buzz Lawrence, was an old friend, and he was a fixture at the Playboy Club. He'd bring me along and it was a real kick hanging with one of Denver's most recognized entertainers. Not to mention that the Playboy Club was a great place to meet folks coming through town. Remember Morey Amsterdam? He used to be on *The Dick Van Dyke Show*, and when he was in town, the Playboy Club was the place to be. We hit it off and soon he would play a big role in my future.

We were playing golf one day and I was talking about Sandra, who worked as a Playboy bunny. I'd met her some time before at a charity promotion for KHOW, while riding around the city on a big open-air truck. It turned out we had grown up only about fifty miles apart in Nebraska. There was something about her, and we just clicked.

I chose one of those rare times when I could have a private conversation with Amsterdam because he was mobbed wherever he went. He was a very funny guy and everyone knew him. He called himself "America's guest" and everyone wanted to play host to the TV celebrity. Amsterdam never disappointed, either. He talked to everyone like they were old friends, and this time on the golf course was a chance to ask his advice.

I just laid it on line. I wasn't really happy with my current situation and I knew I had a future with Sandra, if she wanted a future with me. Here's his advice: "You'd better do what makes you happy. You'd better do what you're going to have to live with for a long time. If you're not happy now, you're not going to be happy when you both go your own way and you'll regret it the rest of your life."

The bottom line? "If that's what you want to do, do it." Turned out to be some of the best advice I ever got. Sandra and I ended up getting married in Las Vegas and honeymooning in Lake Tahoe, and I credit Morey for everything.

A few years later when I got to WGAR, Morey rang me up and said his daughter was marrying a guy from Cleveland. The reception was going to be at Nate's Inner Circle in Beachwood, and Morey said he wanted me at his table. I didn't know any of the family that she was marrying into and neither did Morey, but he needed a friendly face and Sandy and I were safe harbor. We'll always remember Morey! But I'm getting ahead of myself.

So there I was, on top of the world on Denver radio. I even made number one in the ratings for the first time and to honor the occasion, my station manager bought me a Rolex watch that I wore for forty years. I also found out that success can have a short shelf life.

I mentioned "Captain Show Biz." He was the station manager, John Lego. Seriously, he even had a jacket with "Captain Show Biz" on the back. One day my friend Casey Cook pulled me aside and dropped a bombshell: "John, I hate to tell you this but I think Lego is going to fire you."

Cook bought commercial time on the station, so he knew what was going on. He owned a hotel and a couple of restaurants along with Marvelous Marv's, the nightclub where I was hanging out. I was still pretty confident.

"He can't fire me," I said, "I'm number one."

Cook wasn't convinced.

"I don't think that matters to him," he said. "He's going to fire you."

And sure as hell, two days later, he fired me. I never knew why! The only thing I could figure was that he was upset that I wouldn't party with him. He wasn't part of our group. A bunch of us from the station hung out at Marvelous Marv's and "Captain Show Biz" wanted to be part of our group. But I just didn't want to take him along with me. I was pretty much on my own.

I had bought this old Jaguar XKE from Casey Cook and I drove it to work during the day and hung around the club at night. That was my world. It was me, Cook and a couple of other friends from the station like "Hot Dog" Harold Moore and Danny Davis. Lego just wasn't part of it, he didn't like that and, as far as I know, that's why he fired me. The ratings were great and I hadn't been accused of doing anything wrong. He just said, "I think we're going to go in another direction." My time in Denver radio was over.

The funny thing is, the station owners let Lego go not too long after I had left. I was working in Cleveland by then and he flew into town to visit me after he'd been let go. He said he'd like to talk, I said okay, and we went to lunch at Jim Swingo's Keg and Quarter Restaurant. And everybody at the Keg and Quarter came over to me and said, "Hi, how you doing?"

Here's where it gets a little weird. I was doing okay after replacing Don Imus in Cleveland. Lego told me he had a chance at two different jobs, one in Washington and one in San Francisco. Then he asked me if I would come with him!

"I think we could do it together and make it a really good deal," he said.

Wha . . . ?

"YOU FIRED ME!" I shot back. "Why would I go to work for you again? You're nuts!"

"I know," he said, "but this time it will be different."

Right.

"Maybe it will be for you," I said, "but you're not taking me with you."

Eventually he got the hint. After everyone kept coming to our table to say "hi" he said, "You're not leaving here, are you?" Hey, why rub it in? I said, "No, I'm not. But it's nice to talk to you." We talked a few times after that and we remained friends. Lego ended up at a little station in Las Vegas, and that's the last I heard of him.

The point is, he fired me and I ended up in Cleveland. You can say, "What if . . . " but I guess it worked out well in the long run.

But I'm getting ahead of myself here. First, I had to get to Cleveland. Now, about that move . . .

Chapter Three

Coming to Cleveland

WHEN YOU GET THE kind of numbers I had in Denver it draws attention, and I got offers from a friend in Seattle and a station in Dallas. Cleveland turned out to be a good choice.

Don Imus had been at WGAR for maybe a year when he landed a gig at WNBC in New York. He told NBC he was making like $65,000 a year, and he was really making about $19,000 in Cleveland. But they bought it, and gave him more money and took him to New York.

Jack Thayer was the general manager at WGAR in Cleveland, and he heard about me at a convention in New Orleans. He rang me up and told me he was looking to replace his morning man. Interested? I heard that about sixty-five guys had applied for the job when Imus left, but Thayer decided to take a chance on me.

"I heard a lot about what you're doing in Dallas," he said. "I think you'd be perfect for the job."

Yeah, but I had just gotten to Dallas! That didn't matter to Thayer.

"Look," he said, "just think about it. We'd like to fly you to Cleveland." So I decided to give it a shot. It was probably the best opportunity in the country because everybody wanted Imus's gig.

He had made a lot of inroads in personality radio at the time and the guy who followed him had big shoes to fill. That vote of confidence from Thayer meant a lot.

It was December 1970. I flew up to Cleveland, and it sure wasn't Dallas weather. It was cold and snowy, but I was used to that from Nebraska. Thayer was a great guy who got a lot of attention in the radio world. He ended up in New York City, where he became the president of NBC Radio. Cleveland would turn into a big stepping stone for both of us. He showed me around town and introduced me to another important guy at the station, the program director, John Lund. We had a great conversation and he said, "We kind of like you. I think you'll be okay here." Those were the words I needed to hear.

I flew back down to Dallas and told Sandy what was happening, but I don't think she was convinced. "But we're barely unpacked!" she said. Yeah, I know, but she didn't understand that these kinds of things happen in radio all the time.

Here's how we left it in Cleveland. Thayer told me, "I'll call you tomorrow night and let you know what we decide." Was I making the right decision? Was I even getting the job? There were no guarantees. So that night I went out and got drunk. I didn't want to be there when Thayer called and, sure enough, he did. Sandy took the message, and Thayer asked, "Will you please have him call me?" I was obviously not in the right frame of mind to call that night, but I did the next day to hear, "We'd like you to come here and take the job." A month later, the van was packed and we were heading north. I think they paid me $16,000 a year.

Don't get me wrong. Dallas was really nice, but it wasn't me, and I didn't like doing afternoons. Plus, I didn't care for the idea of living in a place where the backyards had the people's money drying on their clotheslines.

There was another major reason for the decision.

I just didn't like KRLD. It was a big station, 50,000 watts, and it was the home of the Dallas Cowboys. It was a ratings monster, but I had no chance of doing morning drive because that was all news. It was the only time in my career I did afternoons and that just wasn't me, but that wasn't the only problem. The station was owned by the family of the Dallas mayor, and they didn't like my style. I tried to be a little outrageous here and there and that brought in ratings, but after the show I'd get called into the program director's office. Here's what those meetings were like:

"Well, the mayor's wife was driving to work and heard you say some things that she didn't quite agree with."

"I'm not here to please the mayor's wife!" I replied, laying it on the line.

"You know what can happen," the program director warned. "They're not real happy with what you're doing."

And I wasn't real happy working in a very conservative city at a station I didn't like. Don't get me wrong. Opportunity had knocked, and I opened that door wide. And not everyone was a problem at KRLD. The program manager, John Barger, was a good guy and he really stood up for me in the meetings. He fought for me but I finally decided that it didn't matter anymore. I was going to Cleveland. After I spoke to Thayer, I walked into Barger's office and said, "I'm sorry, but I'm quitting."

"But you just got here," he said. "How can you quit?"

"You know what? Everything I do on the air, somebody seems to have a complaint about it. Or is upset about it or doesn't like it. I don't want to work for the mayor's family. I know KRLD is a legendary station and you don't want anybody to rock the boat, but I'm really not the right guy for you."

Cleveland, here I come.

And what a reception when I arrived: the city was in the middle of a huge snow storm. It wasn't the weather that bothered me, though. I was more concerned with replacing Don Imus. Gut check. I told myself, *You just got fired in Denver, you went to Dallas and quit after a short time there and didn't like it, and now you're in Cleveland. If you fail here, what are you going to do?*

At WGAR, I lucked out. Thayer backed me up the whole way. He was always there, cheering me on, saying, "You're doing great!" When the ratings finally came out, we were actually doing better than Imus had done. Plus, I had other gigs. One of the reasons the ratings had gone up was because I started doing the *Prize Movie* on WUAB (more on that in a bit). I also had learned that you had to know the community, so I got to know Cleveland Mayor Ralph Perk and put him on the air.

This was turning into a good gig and a really fun experience! It gave me a chance to do what I did without people calling me and telling me not to do this or not to say that. The station management just told me to get in the studio, do what you do and we'll see how it works. I knew there were boundaries, but I wasn't trying to outdo Imus. He'd done a lot of crazy stuff, so you couldn't really break any rules because he'd broken them all anyway. I also had a greater incentive.

It all boiled down to this: I just hoped that I could make it. It was the fear of failure that really drove me the whole time. Thayer was an important ally, even after he went on to NBC. I was concerned about him, too. He wasn't in really great health after he left, and whenever I flew into New York we'd go to brunch on Sunday mornings with his new wife. There was nobody else in my whole life who did more for me in radio than he did. Thayer had brought Imus to town from Sacramento, and then me from Dallas. Everyone came out ahead.

I mentioned that Thayer had stayed in touch even after he had headed to NBC. Here's an example:

Once he was flying from New York to the west coast and in

This huge billboard was painted on the side of a building next to the Innerbelt bridge downtown. See the tiny scaffold at the lower right with two people on it? We we were broadcasting live while hanging there. Morning commuters got a real kick out of it.

those days they carried *Parade Magazine* on the planes. They used to have a comedian's jokes on the back of the cover, and he tore that page out and he circled the jokes that he thought I should use. He'd been gone from Cleveland for a while but he still took the time to send me that page, saying, "Here, these are some good jokes you might like." I never forgot that.

The WGAR studios were in North Royalton in those days, and eventually Thayer took the gig at NBC. I was hoping I'd end up in New York more than anything else so I could work with him again, but there were a few road bumps. Imus was there and eventually Howard Stern was, too, so there really wasn't any place for me

Even so, when I came to Cleveland we had all kinds of people who went on to national fame. Cleveland was the big time to me, and everything I'd heard about the city from Joe Finan seemed to be true. Here's an example:

I'd already been in town for a few years, and I can remember doing several promotions with the new weather guy at WKYC. He was great fun. One time we were at a Cleveland television awards dinner and he and I came out singing "Ebony and Ivory." Of course, it was Al Roker, who also became a national media figure in New York City. There were so many really amazing people that were part of the scene back then.

It wasn't too long before I realized I'd made the right move leaving Dallas for Cleveland. And, believe me, it wasn't for the money. They only paid me $16,000 to replace Don Imus (who was now making $65,000 in New York). Still, it was a big change from when I started out, making a couple hundred dollars a week in Scottsbluff, Nebraska.

Chapter Four

Friends in High Places

WGAR WAS A 50,000-WATT blowtorch. That's radio lingo for a station that didn't have other stations interfering, and "the friendly station" could be heard in 38 states and a big part of Canada during certain times of the day. We gave them plenty to listen to as well. Every day part had a jock who put on a show like morning drive. Lots of interviews, impressions, jingles and a staff who could pull it off. All the shows had comedy bits and lots of telephone calls. It was personality-driven radio, and that was happening all over the country: WLS in Chicago, KOMA in Oklahoma City, and others.

There were a lot of great people at the station. The crossover at 10 a.m. with Joe Mayer came about by accident. Joe was a Cleveland legend when WHK was a Top 40 monster. We would talk at the end of my show sometimes and I would throw a few jokes at him. He'd laugh and take over, and I would leave. As time went on, I threw more at him and he laughed more and it became a daily bit, a big part of the show. Joe Mayer could laugh like no other!

We had taped bits like "Buzz and Juggs" about some geeky teenagers, and "Santa Hanukkah from Santa Monica" was a

Jewish version of Kris Kringle. I believe Jan Jones and Bill Ward were part of the Buzz and Juggs bit. It was all produced locally.

Ah, the Flex Club. We wanted to say the Sex Club, but you couldn't say that on the air in those days. I started that in Albuquerque by playing David Rose's song "The Stripper" at 7 a.m. It was a crazy thing: "It's the Flex Club folks! Get it up, get it on, get ready, get to work." Then I took the Flex Club with me to Denver and we started adding in letters that people sent us to read on the air. We got a lot of mail, so we would read them over the music, using the song as a bed. Eventually people started calling in to the show to talk about it, and the bit kept getting longer and longer. It was supposed to be a minute lead-in to news, and it was going five minutes! At one point we even had Flex shampoo sponsor that segment. It ran its course and we had a lot of fun with it, but eventually I just retired it.

Was there a line not to cross on the air? We talked about politics, and relationships, but the line was in your head. George Carlin once had a bit about seven words you could never say on the air, but there was no real line you couldn't cross. We didn't go racist or mock religion. That was radio back then. You knew what you could do without having to say it. Maybe a few times there were guests who went a little too far, but you just restored order and moved on. The lines kept changing anyway. I didn't attack other people. That was something that Howard Stern loved to do years later, but I didn't do that at all. That was just my personal preference. That may be why Howard and Donald Trump became such good buddies on the radio, because they did the same kind of insults. I didn't believe in attacking and insulting other people. Yeah, you can make fun of them and make jokes about them, and we did it about everybody, but never viciously or to insult them.

One thing that I started doing before I left Denver was having the mayor, Bill McNichols, on the show every week. Politicians give you credibility because most of them have been in the city their whole lives. It doesn't matter if you like them or you don't. We actually became friends.

It worked in Denver, so when I went to Cleveland and started on WGAR, I invited Mayor Ralph Perk on the show. He agreed, I got to know him right off the bat and he helped get me known because we had a regular thing on the air. Nobody else on radio at that time was putting politicians on the air. He was on once a week, letting everyone know what was going on. He helped me immensely by getting out the word that I wasn't just some outsider passing through.

Eventually I came to know his whole family, so I kind of got involved in politics through him. If I had a problem, and I had quite a few of them in my early years, I'd call him and he'd help me out. Here's an example:

You have to promote a successful radio show on and off the air. I was asked to be the Grand Marshal for the city of Parma's Fourth of July parade. This was kind of a big deal because I was new in town, and a lot of people still didn't know me. So on the Fourth I pulled up to park next to the mayor's car and a cop told me, "Hey! You can't park here! This is restricted." I tried to tell him I was in the parade, but he came back with, "You still can't park here. You're going to have to go somewhere else, you understand?"

"I'm not going to go anywhere else," I replied. "I'm the Grand Marshal of the parade and I'm going to park here." Well, one thing led to another and before you knew it, he had arrested me. The parade started and I heard someone ask, "Where's John Lanigan? He's supposed to be the Grand Marshal."

The next thing I knew, I was at the Parma jail with one phone call. Who you gonna call? Not Ghostbusters. They were still a few years away. So I rang up Ralph Perk and gave him a thumbnail account.

"Sorry, John," he said, "I can't do anything for you. I'm heading to the airport and I'm flying out in about two hours to go to Washington, D.C. to see the President."

Uh-oh. Now what?

Perk must have felt sorry for me. He called somebody, who called somebody else, and the next thing I know the jail door opened and the cops said, "We're sorry about this. You can go now." The parade had gone on without me.

I also became friends with the guy who replaced Perk, Dennis Kucinich. Still am.

We had him on the air a lot when he was running for mayor, so when he was elected he told me that he wanted me to be on the dais with him for his swearing-in ceremony at Cleveland Music Hall. I didn't understand why.

"I'm not a politician," I said. "I'm just some radio guy."

"You were part of it," Kucinich responded.

And he wanted me to speak!

"I don't have anything to say! "I protested, but Kucinich stood his ground. Then I had an idea. "If I have to do it, I have to do it my way," I told him.

Deal!

They had a number of people up on the dais and they had me sitting next to Louis Stokes, the congressmen, and former Mayor Carl Stokes's brother. They had quite a lineup of people speaking on behalf of the new mayor, and they brought Stokes up after two or three speakers. I was supposed to be next, but I ducked out of sight and changed into a court jester's outfit. The whole suit, and it looked pretty good. So Stokes finished up and went back to his seat and the master of ceremonies introduced me, but I was nowhere to be found. He didn't seem pleased.

"That's just like those media people," he said. "They're never on time and they're never prepared when we're ready." As he was saying those words I casually strolled out to the podium as a court

At the inauguration ceremony for Cleveland Mayor Dennis Kucinich on November 15, 1977, I appeared wearing a court jester outfit—to show that Cleveland was tired of being a national joke. My outfit and speech were included in a *New York Times* article about Kucinich. *(Akron Beacon Journal)*

jester. The place exploded! I told him I would do it my way, and had a good reason behind it.

My idea was that Cleveland had been a joke for too long. We were tired of being made fun of as the "mistake on the lake" and all the rest of it. So I stood up at the podium and said, "Well, we got a new guy at City Hall. He's young, he's aggressive and he's going to be interesting. And you know what? We're not going to be laughed at anymore. We're going to laugh back, and that's why I'm up here, to let you know that we're not going to take it anymore."

I felt sort of like a renaissance Howard Beale. It got a great response, too. It made it all the way to *The New York Times*. The article was about Kucinich's election, but it also mentioned the court jester who said we're not going to be laughed at anymore. You can laugh at me, but not the city.

Good Morning America came into town in 1981 to do their show from the top of our West 6th Street studio building. (Left to right) David Hartman, host of GMA; me; Dayton's Erma Bombeck, a national columnist; Akron's Tom Batiuk, creator of the comic strip *Funky Winkerbean*.

We've stayed friends over the years and have been involved in a lot of other things together. Oddly enough, people forget that he ran for president twice. You'd see him during the Democratic debates with all the other big candidates. Hey, he might have been the outsider who didn't have much of a chance, but there he was. Gotta give him credit for that!

Kucinich had had a pretty tough life. He once told me that he wanted to sell his house in Washington, D.C., and move back to Cleveland. I said, "You've come a long way from living in your car, haven't you?" You know, at one point in his life he actually was living in his car. He didn't have anywhere to live. He just kind of smiled and he said, "You're right, John. I have come a long way." He made it a point to call me on my last day at WMJI. He was stuck at Fox News in Washington, but I sure appreciated that call.

Chapter Five

Wild and Crazy Stunts

RADIO PEOPLE WANT TO be in the public eye as well as in the ear, and throughout my career I pulled off a lot of what I like to call "crazy stunts." They were really just promotions for the station, but the more outrageous they were, the more you were seen. This was typical of the radio biz, and the stunts were usually during the ratings periods. Those were the days when radio stations competed for listeners to jack up their Arbitron ratings. Even a promotion that had listeners buzzing for a day or two would help. It's simple math. The higher the ratings, the more money the station could charge its advertisers. So we were all called upon to do a promotion now and then, and the wilder and crazier, the better.

When I first came to Cleveland I had a good impression of the place. There were fun places to go, lots of clubs and restaurants, and even more now. So one of the first promotions I did when I came to Cleveland was in the Flats, the entertainment district that had sprung up along the banks of the Cuyahoga River near Lake Erie. The businesses there wanted publicity to drive folks to come down.

Jerry Powell had a nightclub called Pickle Bill's near the mouth of the Cuyahoga River. Diana Nyad was in the news then for swimming from Florida to Cuba, surrounded by a metal cage pulled by a boat to guard her from the sharks. So we decided to have some fun with it and do the same thing, only I was going to swim across the Cuyahoga in a carp cage to save me from fish that are pretty harmless. We went to Pickle Bill's and built this silly carp cage and word got around pretty quickly. It turned into a big promotion. Now, keep in mind the Cuyahoga River still had an international reputation as the river that had caught fire back in 1969.

We put the cage in the water and all the six o'clock news television cameras were there to cover it live. They watched me dive into the Cuyahoga and get into the carp cage, and then a boat pulled it in front of me as I swam. It was a great promotion—in theory.

I almost drowned! I kept swallowing water and the river was still polluted. Really polluted! It wasn't a good thing to ingest Cuyahoga River water. I admit, I had been warned. Everybody told me, "You're nuts, you'll get sick, you'll die. Whatever." Okay, I did get sick from taking in water, but it was still a fun promotion. We kind of set the tone for what we were going to do in the coming weeks and months, fun things like that. And that's what we did.

One of my scariest radio stunts was when I was asked to help open the annual Cleveland Air Show at Burke Lakefront Airport. The promotions department wanted me to go up in a parasail. There's an area of water between the breakwall and the shore where boats anchor to watch the air show, and they have bleachers set up on the runway where the spectators can watch the planes go by. One of the show's sponsors, a parasailing company, wanted to pull me up in the air behind a boat to open the show. Like an idiot, I agreed!

Here was the plan: I would be coming over the water next to the shore from east to west, right in front of the bleachers. I actually took off from the land, not from the water, on a pair of skis, as

I know this photo is from a publicity stunt in Colorado, but I can't remember which one. There were a lot of them!
(Akron Beacon Journal)

After the parasailing accident over Lake Erie. My wife, Sandy, had to push me around in a wheelchair after the accident put my leg in a cast. But I didn't miss a broadcast, thanks to Sandy driving me to and from work.

you'd imagine. I guess it's a common way of doing that. Nothing unusual, but the problem was that they needed someone driving the boat who had some idea about what he was doing. Uh oh . . .

As the driver pulled me along in front of the shore, my parasail kept dipping, going up and coming back down. At that point I was pretty close to the breakwall. I could tell that I was in trouble because the driver didn't seem to know exactly how to keep me up. He kept varying his speed and I started to get really scared. I realized he didn't have any control of me zipping around up there, and I didn't know where I was going—but I found out pretty quick.

The boat swerved and swung around and I was headed right at the breakwall! There's no doubt that if I'd hit the wall, it would have killed me, but at the last minute he pulled away and turned me around. I did crash, but luckily it was into the water. It got worse.

My leg was facing the wrong way, and my knee was pretty badly torn up, although we didn't know that at the time. As I hit the water my leg got twisted in the wrong direction, and I had to swim back to the boat. After I got on board the driver took me in and dropped me off, and I really wasn't sure what had happened, but it wasn't good.

My knee was a mess. Instead of bending backward and forward, it moved sideways. Ligaments were torn all over the place. I managed to get back to my car and called my wife, Sandy. I told her that I was hurt and didn't know what to do. She was somewhere else, so I said I'd meet her at home.

I'm not sure how but I was able to drive my car home. It was the left leg but I had a stick shift and I had to push down on the clutch to put it in gear. It hurt like hell. Still, I got it into gear, got the car home and Sandy took me to the hospital, where they took care of it. What a promotion, and that wasn't the end of it.

I don't think I ever heard again from the people who had asked me to parasail for them. They said they were going to use that stunt to advertise, but they never did inquire about me to see how I was doing after I went to the hospital. My knee wasn't right for a long time after that.

One of my favorite stunts was when I flew with the U.S. Air Force Thunderbirds to publicize the air show. The Thunderbirds are a crack team who do stunts at air shows across the country. Quite a thrill! They would come into town and ask media people if they'd like to go up and fly with them before the air show opened. This was some flight, too. One year they asked me to go on a demo flight and I jumped at the chance. You take a little sit-down test and go through some stuff and then they put you in a plane and take you up with them. They generally fly you to Dayton, then turn around and come back. At top speed, it's a short flight. Believe me, they're moving.

So you go on this high-speed flight to Wright Patterson Air Force Base in Dayton and back. You do the rolls and upside-down turns, all those kind of things that give you a feeling of what it's all about. It was really a thrill and after it was over, they took a couple of pictures of me standing by the jet. Publicity shots, hand-shakes and then you go back and talk about it on the air. It was a PR thing for them. But some people don't know what they're in for and get plenty sick when the pilots start doing stunts. I didn't, because I had a bit of experience flying, and had even taken flying lessons for a while in Albuquerque, but I never finished getting my license.

I really enjoyed flying with the Thunderbirds. The next year the Blue Angels came into town. They're U.S. Navy pilots who do the same gig as the Thunderbirds. Word had gotten around about my trip with the Thunderbirds and they said they'd like me to try it with them this time. They'd done it with somebody from New

Settling into the cockpit of a U.S. Air Force jet. I flew with the Thunderbirds as a promotion for the annual Cleveland Air Show in 1979. I sat behind Captain Jim Jiggens, the pilot.

York the week before, one of the guys from the *Today* show, and they had heard about me. No hesitation. I said, "Yeah, I'll do it again."

So Sandy came with me to the airport, I got into one of the Navy planes and did basically the same thing that I had done with the Thunderbirds, flying to Dayton and back. When you turn around there sometimes they do a quick touchdown before they come back. You don't really do a full stop there. They're just having fun.

They did all the upside down and flying around and so on like the Thunderbirds, and when we flew back to Burke I thought we were done. Not yet. They decided to make this flight a little different. They just didn't bother to tell me.

The pilots did a thing called a "push up to landing." We came into Burke Airport as if we were about to land but just when we were almost right on the ground, the pilot flew clear to the end of the runway, throttled up and *whooosh!* —the jet shot straight up at about a 90-degree angle, soaring like a rocket. I didn't expect that, and my stomach started doing somersaults! And of course you can't throw up in your helmet or you'll have an even bigger problem.

I knew they were messing with me and, no doubt about it, they got me good. From what Sandy said she heard back at the airport, they were having a big laugh over the whole thing because they knew they had nailed me. Sandy could hear them laughing back and forth, as she was listening to their radio talk. They said, "You think you did good last time? Well, let me show you what it's really all about." I guess I found out, all right!

They do those "push up to landings" all the time, but if you're prepared for it and you know what's going on, it's okay. It's when you're sitting in the second seat behind the pilot and he flies in, goes right across the runway, and suddenly goes straight up at full throttle that it's all over. I never really recovered from it. I had never gotten airsick before, but after that I've had a number of flights that I've been on, even on commercial flights, where I did. I don't throw up, but I get nauseated. Thanks a lot, Blue Angels! At least I got to fly with them. But I wouldn't do it again.

A lot of our stunts were inspired by whatever was happening in the news. One time there was this guy, Steve Fossett, who flew a hot-air balloon all the way around the world. It was big news at the time. I was into hot-air balloons because of my radio stint in Albuquerque. That's where hot-air balloon shows were just beginning to take off. They're really a big deal there now. Every year they have this giant show and the balloons just get wilder and wilder.

We thought we'd do our own Cleveland version. Our version

would be a little different. It was supposed to be this silly promotional stunt where we fly a hot-air balloon across Lake Erie. Of course, we didn't know what we were doing and, as usual, that was a mistake.

We found a pretty reputable balloon company in Cleveland, and they said they'd try it, but we'd probably be going the wrong way. I figured it could be fun; we would see what happens. I had done some hot-air balloon rides in New Mexico, so I knew how to ride them. I figured it would be fun even if we went in the wrong direction. In hindsight, that might have not been the best approach.

One of the problems with that idea is that when you're flying north across Lake Erie, you're flying against the main direction of the wind. A hot-air balloon would really travel best going from west to east. We thought we'd have some fun with it anyway.

Rick Case Honda was a big sponsor on our show, and Rick was a friend of mine, so we asked him to follow us in his boat in case we crashed in the middle of Lake Erie. It was good to know there'd be a boat out there if we needed it. There were three of us, including the balloon pilot and a reporter, Tappy Phillips from WEWS, who came along on the ride to cover it. Phillips would go on to a big career in New York City, but this time around she came along to help promote Channel 5.

As soon as we took off, the balloon had a mind of its own.

Rick took off in his boat to follow us, but we later found out somebody had sabotaged it by putting sugar in his gas tank! Really, that's what they found in his gas tank later on. It wasn't long before his boat was dead in the water and had to be towed back to shore.

So we found ourselves with no boat to back us up and we were going in the wrong direction. You can't fight the winds. We were going east instead of north to Canada, and ended up floating

I tried to ride a hot-air balloon across Lake Erie from Cleveland to Canada as a radio promotion. I ended up in a field in Pennsylvania.

around until we finally came down in a field somewhere in Pennsylvania. The whole trip was a disaster.

After we landed we got to a phone and told the balloon company to come and get us. You usually have these chase cars that follow you wherever you go. Then they come and pick up the balloon. But it was hard following us over the lake. They finally found us and everyone got home safely.

Dan Striepeke, the makeup artist from the movie *Planet of the Apes*, gave me my own ape face. We did it in the May Company store window on Public Square as the public watched. Circa 1974. *(Courtesy of WJW TV)*

Despite that episode, I still love hot-air balloons. At one point I was even thinking about getting one.

Here's another story about flying with a much happier ending. Bill Randle was someone I idolized. When I came to Cleveland I thought to myself that this was where Bill Randle worked, and I was quite taken by him. Huge fan. It wasn't long after I got here that I got a call from Randle, who was off the air and teaching at Kent State.

"Hey, you sound good and I'm listening to you," he said. "I'm teaching broadcast classes here at Kent State. Would you consider coming here to talk to my students?"

I didn't have anything prepared and had never really done anything like that, but anything Bill wanted, I was going to do, just to finally meet him. He said it was a question-and-answer session and they would ask about breaking into the business. Just talk to them, have a good time and that would be it. I said I would be glad to.

"Tell you what I'll do," Bill said. "I'll pick you up." He told me to go to the Cuyahoga County Airport, where he had his own plane. On top of everything, he was a private pilot, and he flew me to Kent State. I did the whole class with him, and we talked a lot and got to know each other. Then we flew back to my car. What an experience! I was absolutely thrilled. He was a legend in our business and here he was, befriending me.

After that we would talk now and then. A few years later, Bill was inducted into the Ohio Broadcasters Hall of Fame. I got a phone call from Bill and he said it was a nice honor, but no big deal. Then he asked, "Would you introduce me?" I thought for a moment. Out of all the amazing people that Bill Randle knows, he called me to introduce him. I was stunned. Flattered and stunned and surprised and everything else. Of course I said yes, and I started doing as much research as I could about him. I found out he'd had a club in Detroit and his bodyguard had been Malcolm X (he used the name Detroit Red at that time). I thought after I had introduced Bill that you don't do much better than that.

I was able to promote the morning show on WGAR and the *Prize Movie* on stage, too. I wanted to act a little bit. Years before I had done *Everybody's Girl* onstage in Albuquerque with Vivian Vance from the *The Lucy Show*. It was written by John Patrick, who'd won a Pulitzer for *Teahouse of the August Moon*. I got to know them both fairly well, and Patrick said, "Why don't you come do a show?" I had done some theater in high school, but not much. I was the only guy in *Oklahoma* who didn't sing! I was the peddler man, the only non-singing role. I tried it and liked it, and when I got to Cleveland the director of the Huntington

Playhouse asked me to be in a few shows. There was one with Stu Levin, *The Odd Couple*, that was a huge hit.

Oh, one more thing about Rick Case. We did another publicity stunt with him that was really fun at the Richfield Coliseum during the halftime show of some event. It could have been a Cavs game. It was a demolition derby and we only used Hondas, since that's what Case sold, and he made it a point to kick it up a notch. About half a dozen radio and TV personalities were each given their own cars. We rode them around the track, doing the demolition derby thing, and it was fun. We were going at a safe speed so no one was risking injury or anything like that.

So we were crashing into each other and suddenly the announcer yelled out, "Ladies and gentlemen, here's Rick Case." The crowd started cheering when he came out driving a semi-truck cab. He rolled down the ramp and onto the court and drove around the whole Coliseum track in the semi.

That was the point where we all said, "Okay we're out of here." None of us wanted to mess with Case and his semi. It was really funny and the crowd loved it.

Over the years we did lot of those kinds of stunts or promotions or whatever you want to call them and they were all a good time—when they went as planned!

Chapter Six

Prize Movie

GOOD THINGS HAPPENED WHEN I came to Cleveland, and one of the best was the *Prize Movie*. So what's a prize movie? In 1971 I was wondering the same thing. It was the early afternoon movie show on WUAB-TV, back when there were only a few channels on television. You had the big three: WEWS (Channel 5, the ABC affiliate), WKYC (Channel 3, which was NBC) and WJW (Channel 8, and they carried CBS programming). Then you had a few ultrahigh frequency (UHF) channels such as WUAB, Channel 43, that were the early ancestors of cable television. WVIZ was the PBS outlet for programs like *Sesame Street*.

I had watched the *Prize Movie* a few times because I had my afternoons off after I did my morning show, but I never paid much attention to it until the day I took a fateful bike ride. Sandy and I were living in the Ledgewood Townhouses in Strongsville when we first came here from Denver. It was quick drive to the WGAR studios in Broadview Heights.

So one afternoon I was out for a bike ride and a guy pulled his bike up alongside mine. We got to talking and he introduced himself as Jack Moffitt, the general manager at WUAB. He told me his *Prize Movie* host, Jack Reynolds, was quitting to take a radio spot on WWWE (now WTAM). It was the afternoon slot so Reynolds couldn't do both. But maybe I could because I was doing mornings. He asked me if I'd ever done any television and I told him I had been a TV weatherman for four years out west. It just so happened that they were auditioning for his replacement the very next day.

"Why don't you come down tomorrow and give it a shot?" Moffitt asked.

I showed up, along with a bunch of hopefuls, including one lady who was auditioning with her dog. I did my little piece and afterward they took me into the office.

"We think you'd be perfect for it," Moffitt said. "Would you want to do it?" I thought it was worth a try. Then he dropped this on me. "Well, can you start tomorrow?"

Tomorrow was as good as any other day.

I wasn't expecting much, but as promised, I started the next day and ended up staying for more than twenty years. Trust me, I didn't do it for the money. They only paid me $25 a show, but it gave me a lot of free publicity. Plus, because it was a regional channel, it linked up with other channels and satellites like a cable station. The show was broadcast all over Ohio, New York, Canada and Western Pennsylvania. We were almost like a superstation. We gave them plenty to watch, and it gave me something to do. I knew too many morning radio guys with nothing to do the rest of the day. They ended up drinking a lot, and that wasn't for me.

It also opened up a lot of other opportunities for me. I would get paid for doing live commercials and endorsements. Then I started doing nightclub appearances. It was a real godsend. That was the power of television.

This is how the *Prize Movie* worked. Viewers would send in postcards and we'd pick one out of a barrel. We got postcards

TV talk show host Steve Allen joined me on the set of *Prize Movie*. Guests would pick a name out of the letter bin next to me and we would call them on the phone.

from all over Ohio, New York, Canada, everywhere. Then we'd call the sender on the phone and spin an upright roulette wheel like the one on *Wheel of Fortune*.

The viewer would have to name the face on the picture that the wheel landed on. If they guessed correctly they would have to name a movie from an obscure film clip. If they got it right, they won a cash prize. Our guest celebrity would spin the wheel like Vanna White, and I've been asked if they got the idea from us or us from them, but I'm not sure. If no one was home when we called, we would go to break and try again. If the viewer didn't know the clip, we would add $5 to the jackpot. Sometimes the jackpot grew to big bucks, too, like $500.

Our running joke was that our audience was almost completely men. The women back then watched the soap operas that were on the big three channels. We had guys who were either off work, sick, or unemployed, and they didn't care if the movies were mostly crap which, let's face it, they were. We ran the stuff that wasn't good enough for later in the evening.

My favorite *Prize Movie* story involved this movie clip that no one could get right. All you saw was this kid looking up and saying "Is that the tree?" It was from a fairly well-known movie but no one could guess it. The guessing went on forever, and the pot grew to more than a thousand dollars. Then the gossip columnist for the *Plain Dealer*, Mary Strassmeyer, gave away the answer in her column. Someone had told her it was from the movie *A Man Alone*. So she wrote in her column that she was sick of the clip and hoped someone would please get rid of it. I thought that would be it, but you know what? They still couldn't get it right! Maybe it was because a lot of the postcards were from out of town and those people didn't read her column. It took another month before someone got it. It even became a catch phrase. People would walk around saying, "Is that the tree?" to each other.

Sometimes when we called, the guy who had sent the card was now back to work and a relative would answer. So we put that person on the show instead. We were also watched by a lot of retired couples who sent in cards that said: "Say 'hi' to the crew."

Suddenly people could put a face to the Lanigan voice they heard on the radio. It made me recognizable. I couldn't go anywhere in Northeast Ohio without someone saying, "Hey Lanigan, how you doing?" Even on my trips abroad I'd run into people who knew my face. I remember visiting a cemetery in Moscow, and a guy came up to me and said, "Hey Lanigan, what's on the *Prize Movie* today?" That one made me laugh.

The best part of the movie was the guests we had on. A lot of famous people came by. If you were in the spotlight and people were talking about you, we'd try to get you on the air. One time Arnold Schwarzenegger stopped by and made the phone calls for us. He was just starting his acting career and he'd call folks and say, "Hello, this is Arnold." They wouldn't believe him.

Ted Turner came to the studio when we were doing the *Prize Movie* and he sat there for a while watching it. He had just taken over WTBS in Atlanta and wanted to make it a national station. He also wanted to do a movie in the afternoon. Turner kind of used the *Prize Movie* as an example of what he wanted to do, and I let him know, "I'm available! I'm available!" He didn't listen to me. Turner did start a movie program on 'TBS that had breaks in it and gave prizes. It ran for quite a while before they changed the format.

Another *Prize Movie* guest was Bill Graham, the guy who created the famous Fillmore auditoriums in New York and San Francisco. Just about every major rock artist played there, including John Lennon. Graham was promoting a movie about the Fillmores.

Chuck Barris came on to plug *The Gong Show Movie*. He seemed a lot calmer without the gong. Steve Allen, the great nighttime talk show host, stopped by once. He was famous for his "man-on-the-street interviews" in New York City, and he did one in front of our station on Day Drive behind Parmatown Mall. Cars were driving by, honking their horns, and one guy even stuck his head out the window and hollered, "Holy crap, is that Steve Allen?"

Another favorite guest was Marilyn Chambers, the porn actress who embarrassed the folks at Proctor and Gamble when it was discovered that she had appeared on their Ivory Snow detergent box as a baby. She was in town to promote her infamous XXX movie, *Behind the Green Door*. Back then there was a movie theatre downtown that only showed porn movies when they became fashionable. It was very reputable. Even couples would

On the set of *Prize Movie* with actor George Hamilton. He gave away a television set and some Cotton Club soda pop. *(Courtesy of WUAB TV)*

go there, and Marilyn was a big star in the industry. She was a fun guest and we joked around a lot. I told the audience, "Yes, this is the real Marilyn Chambers and, yes, her movie is showing downtown, and yes, we will talk to her more in a minute." She also caused an awkward moment on the set.

We had gone to a commercial break. I was talking to her and then Gary, the director in another room, said, "Okay, John, coming back in five, four, three, two, one." I looked around and Marilyn was gone! She had dropped below the panel we were standing behind. She popped back up, looked at the camera with a sexy grin and said, "Oh, my god, are we back on?" *Whoa!* I told her, "Don't ever do that to me again." But she was having fun with it. You couldn't get away with that nowadays. It was iffy even back then.

We had a lot of entertainers and athletes on the show, but the difference between us and daytime talk shows is that we didn't interview them. They just spun the wheel, played the game, and had some fun.

The crew was a big part of the show, too. We had a running gag in which cameraman Brian Johnson's hand would come into the shot and grab some stuff. Just his hand, that's all you ever saw, like "Thing" on the old *Addams Family* show. Every now and then the crew would pull practical jokes on me, too. Here's one: They got sick of me complaining about the snow all the time. They put a guy up in the grid with one of those snow machines and as soon as I complained about the snow they turned it on. The audience loved it, and I will admit that gag was one of the better ones.

Then there was the time when pieces of the Skylab were falling from outer space, and it was in the news. The crew took a garbage can and filled it with soft junk and attached it to a rope over my head. Then they tricked me into mentioning the Skylab and when I did, they dropped the junk on me. Captain Kangaroo did that with balloons, but my audience was a little older. It was a great atmosphere to work in. We were like a family, and the audience could see it.

One of the all-time great guests was Alan Bean, the famous astronaut, who was the fourth man to walk on the moon. We had him on our radio show as well as on the *Prize Movie*. I was once able to spend a day with him when he was in town to publicize some of his paintings that were on display at a local art gallery. He talked about what it was like to be out in space and especially when he was flying the spacecraft behind the moon, where they would be out of contact with the Houston control center. Bean told me he would take the controls and have some fun doing what he wanted with the spacecraft, flying it this way and that way.

"Weren't you afraid you'd like get out of orbit or something and never come back?" I asked.

"That wasn't going to happen," he assured me.

After he retired from NASA, Bean became an incredible painter and he did a show at an east side gallery. He even gave me a numbered lithograph of his painting of a guy in a spacesuit on the moon as thanks for the publicity we had given him. He signed it, "To John, who has traveled almost as much as I have." It is still one of my most prized possessions.

We had big names on the *Prize Movie*! Don Rickles, the comedian who was famous for putting people down, was just the nicest guy in the world. When he stopped by the *Prize Movie* to plug his show at the Front Row Theater, he had fun with the calls and the movie, basically doing what Rickles does so well. We were talking after the movie and I told him that I had tickets for his show, and he said, "Oh great, I'll see you there." I sure didn't expect what was in store that evening.

To be picked on by the great Don Rickles was the ultimate thrill. The Front Row had a revolving stage and Rickles was picking on everybody in the audience. Then the stage came around in front of my section and he saw me in the audience. He stopped what he was doing, walked to the front of the stage and said, "There's that guy from the *Prize Movie*. Oh my god, is that the worst thing on television, or what? I'd rather watch a fly die on a curtain." For a couple of minutes he just beat the living crap out of me. The audience knew the show pretty well so he went on and on about it. He just cut me to ribbons and all I could do was just sit there and take it. There's nothing else you could do when you were the target of Don Rickles. It was just such a kick that when it was over, I thought to myself, that'll stay with me forever. But it wasn't over yet.

When the show ended the usher came over to us and said Rickles wanted us to come back to his dressing room and say "hi." Sandy and I went backstage.

"Hey, how are you?" Rickles asked. "It's good to see you again. I really enjoyed doing your show today. I hope I wasn't too hard on you tonight." Was he kidding? I wouldn't have missed it! That was probably my all-time favorite thing that happened thanks to the *Prize Movie*.

There's an old saying in show business that you don't want to work with kids or animals, and I should have taken that advice. "Jungle Larry" Tetzlaff stopped by one day to talk about his animal exhibit at Cedar Point. He'd been around for years as a regular on the Captain Penny kids' show at WEWS. Larry brought in a live cobra in a glass cage, and when I walked up to look at it, the damn thing snapped at me so fast it scared the crap out of me. Thank god for that glass!

Then there was the guy who brought in a boxing kangaroo. He put boxing gloves on its little arms and I pretended to spar with it. No one had warned me about its long back legs. The kangaroo sat back on its tail and gave me a shot to my crotch with his hind leg that almost crippled me.

I enjoyed having Dan O'Shannon on the *Prize Movie*. Dan made a name for himself in L.A. writing and producing shows like *Newhart, Cheers,* and *Frazier*. But before that, Dan had been a fan of my radio show. He used to write jokes for me when he was in high school in Euclid. I'd use them, and he would record them. When the final episode of *Cheers* was taping, everyone wanted to watch. I was in L.A. that week, and I called to get hold of him about something else. Someone told me, "I'm sorry sir, but the show is ending tonight and the place is a mad house. Dan's very busy right now." I understood, and said, "Just tell him John Lanigan called." A minute later I heard Dan's voice saying, "You want to come? I'll get you seats right down front. I'll take care of it." He sure did! On *Frazier*, the character Frazier Crane was a radio talk-show host in Seattle. Danny called me and told me he was going to add another radio character to the show named John Lanigan. Great—but one problem. He later he called back to say he couldn't do it because there was another real John Lanigan who lived in Seattle and the lawyers were afraid they might be sued. I thanked him for the thought.

Ever heard of Drew Carey? Of course—who hasn't? He sent us jokes, and was on the *Prize Movie* a couple of times. He went on to do *The Drew Carey Show*, which was set in Cleveland. Later on Carey invited me out to L.A. to appear on the show, and I was in one episode in a crowd scene at a bar with comedian John Henton.

When I was doing the *Prize Movie* I was also taping a Sunday night show called *Lanigan at Large*. We taped it during the week when we were doing the *Prize Movie*. The station also sent me along to cover these movie junkets. I talked to people like Charlton Heston and Jack Lemmon, and those interviews showed up on *Lanigan at Large*. It was only a half-hour show, a throwaway show that filled up time on Sunday night. I had fun doing it, but I don't think they thought that much about it. A lot of the people who were on the *Prize Movie* also did segments on *Lanigan at Large*.

Prize Movie did a lot for my career. It even did great when I was on vacation. One time my morning show partner, Jimmy Malone, took over for me, and guess who his celebrity guest was? Halle Berry.

What a week to take a vacation!

Chapter Seven

The Tampa Experiment

I WORKED AT WGAR IN Cleveland for about 13 years and, thankfully, it didn't take long to make everyone forget Don Imus. I read somewhere that before long we had almost doubled his ratings but I find that hard to believe. We were doing pretty well, though. Even so, by 1984, like they say, "the times they were a'changing." Most cars now had FM receivers and the AM band was dying fast.

One day I got a call from two guys who owned WIXY 1260 in Cleveland, Norman Wain and Bob Weiss. They were a big part of Cleveland radio history, and they offered me an FM job in Tampa, Florida, as the morning guy on WMGG. I could see the writing on the wall for the AM stations, and I accepted the offer. It was pretty nice to go from Cleveland's climate to Tampa, where it was warm and sunny and you had all the beaches. I made the decision to go to Florida basically to get out of the contract back in Cleveland. I don't know if that station was where I expected to end up, but it was fun and the weather was great.

Let me stress that I never felt like an outsider from up north. Everyone in Florida is from somewhere else. The old timers I met back then are still good friends. It really didn't have an effect on me one way or another.

Radio in Tampa could be boring in a lot of ways, but it soon became highly competitive. There was a time when they brought in London and Engleman in the morning, and there was the Q Morning Zoo, Dave and Dave on the alternative station, Jack Harris, who's still in Tampa, and my show. That's five heavy-hitting morning shows going after the numbers for a tourist market! All those people have since left, but for about six months, it was front page news all the time, whatever you did. You had to come up with outrageous things to do to get publicity. At that time it was radio. It's what radio was all about.

I made it a point not to make Cleveland jokes when I was in Tampa. I talked about Cleveland with fondness and said that I had had a great time working there and had made lots of friends. I wasn't going to fall into the trap of making jokes about a place that had been very good to me.

Back in Cleveland, someone started a drive to try to bring me back to town. Mary Strassmeyer—remember her?—"Mary, Mary" in the *Plain Dealer*? She wanted to write about it. She got hold of people in Tampa Bay and Clearwater and interviewed them, trying to find out what I had said about Cleveland—if I had put it down. She was trying to claim that I didn't deserve to return.

It got back to me what Mary was trying to do, to smear me in the paper for putting Cleveland down, but there was no story because it had never happened.

I enjoyed Florida—the boating and weather—and I made a lot of friends. What was not to like? But it wasn't going to be where I spent the rest of my radio career. I wound up staying only for about a year and a half.

I gave it a good shot, though.

The first thing we did was to try to pump up the ratings with some promotions like we had done at the other stations where I'd worked. I got the idea for the first one when I stopped by a hotel bar that was by the beach. This really attractive bartender was pouring drinks and she had a bucket on the bar that read, "Barb's Bust Fund." She wanted to get her breasts enlarged, and was saving up for implants. A light bulb went off, and I thought that would be kind of a fun promotion. We went on the air with a bit where we offered to help Barb get bigger breasts. We basically opened it up to the audience, asking them to contribute to her bust fund—and they did, big time. And the ball kept rolling from there.

A plastic surgeon who did breast implants called in and volunteered to do it free. Then we got an outpatient medical facility to give us the space free as well. The doctor and the medical facility both wanted to be part of the promotion. Oh, and the donations: We used that money to pay for any added expenses that might occur. They put it all together, we put it on the air and had a lot of fun with it. Barb got her breasts implants and it was win-win-win, all the way around. We even had a coming-out party at the bar, so people could come in and see how good she looked, and what they had gotten for their money. Barb met a guy during the party and they hit it off. The last I heard, she had married him and moved away.

She got what she wanted and we got a lot of publicity because it was an outrageous promotion for a radio station, to give away breasts on the air. Some people thought it was trashy and some people thought it was funny, but it did cause some talk and it got us a write-up in the paper. That's what it's all about.

Another one we did in Tampa was inspired by the time the Russians were trying to figure out who was in charge of their country. Their leader, Konstantin Chernenko, had disappeared and no one knew whether he was dead or alive. The two previous Soviet leaders had died during the past two years. So we started a promotion based on the story. We asked the listeners to guess the date the Soviets would announce Chernenko's death. He was 73 years old and seemed to have been in extremely poor health. I told the local newspaper that every time he appeared in public he looked as if Jim Henson, the puppeteer from the Muppets, was holding him up.

Whenever the Soviets finally broke the news, we would hold a drawing among all the contestants who had submitted the correct answer. I offered to take the winner on a free trip to Moscow. The promotion was called "To Russia With Lanigan." But if you didn't want to go to Russia you could win a new videocassette recorder and a copy of the James Bond movie *To Russia With Love*. Those were the days when VCRs carried a hefty price tag, so it was a pretty serious prize. We even offered runners-up caviar and bottles of vodka. I told the paper that the contest would end when Chernenko did. Some of their readers thought it was in poor taste to bet on someone's death, but we had fun with it.

Somebody actually won, too! It turned out that Chernenko was alive but unable to serve anymore. We decided that counted. But the guy who won the trip said, "I don't want to go to Russia! I'm afraid of Russia. I'll take the video." That VCR cost a lot less than a plane ticket, hotel, and a weekend of latkes and borscht. It turned out to be a pretty inexpensive promotion that made the front page of the Clearwater paper and got us a lot of good publicity.

A boat promotion stirred up some real interest. There was a partially sunken boat in the bay between Clearwater Beach and Tampa under a long bridge that carried a lot of tourist traffic. It was an eyesore in an otherwise beautiful area, so I started this "Let's get rid of this boat. Whose is it?" promotion. Nobody seemed to know who owned it, and nobody wanted to claim it because then they would have had to haul it away. It was obviously cheaper to leave it there.

Ed Droste is a friend of mine and one of the guys who started the Hooters restaurant chain. The original Hooters is right there on the main street in Clearwater, the road that heads toward that bridge that goes across the bay. Hooters had a boat with its name on it that cruised around the bay. I got Ed to send it out and paint the abandoned wreck, which was sitting there half out of the water, and put a Hooters banner across it.

That finally got the eyesore towed away. But get this: The guy who owned the sunken boat finally spoke up, and he was furious with me for basically hauling his trash.

No matter what we tried, I wasn't a big success in Tampa. It never really worked. They changed the format after I got there, and when things started to happen, they changed it again. We were playing middle-of-the-road music and they were going after the Q Zoo, the big morning show. It was a real battle. I'll talk about it more in the "Radio Wars" chapter, but there were four really hot morning shows back then, which is a lot more than they have in Tampa these days. So we competed and it was fun. But I didn't think the fun was going to last, and I was already looking for another job.

I called an old friend, Jay Cook, who was a vice president of the Gannett media company. He had once tried to hire me for another Tampa station when I was still in Cleveland. I told him it wasn't working for me down here and I didn't know what to do.

"Get the hell out of here, that's what you should do," he said. "Go to a place where people get up in the morning and listen to you. You're in a tourist area where people come and go. They don't care about the radio. The weather is nice and you're not that big of a deal to them and neither is anybody else. Go to some-place like Detroit or Chicago or Cleveland or New York where you get up in the morning and your lives are busy and you're going to work. That's where you become a part of their lives."

I got a call from a station in Detroit about working there. As a courtesy, I asked my boss at WMGG if I could go talk to the Detroit station. But management said no—I was under contract. And soon after, the owners called me and fired me.

They obviously weren't getting what they wanted ratings-wise and they just wanted to cut their costs. And, let's face it, I was a cost. The station never really did much after that. I didn't pay much attention, but everybody I knew was gone in a short period of time, including John Pinch, the manager who had fired me (and who later got a big job at Cumulus Radio). Pinch is now a good friend who lives about five blocks from me in Clearwater Beach. We talked about my firing recently, and he said it didn't work out because they didn't give us enough time. They kept changing the format little by little so it didn't feel like a fit.

It was fun for the time I were there, but ending it didn't break my heart.

And then I got a call from the "Diamond Man."

Larry Robinson owned the J.B. Robinson Co. jewelry store chain in Cleveland. He was a big-time radio advertiser, and his commercials made him famous locally. He also owned radio stations, including WMJI-FM.

"You have to come back here," Larry said. "Come back to Cleveland and we'll work it out."

I had met with three or four stations, and Sandy and I talked it over. I had a few other offers, but Robinson's sounded the best, and I decided to take it. We were heading back to Cleveland.

Tampa had been an interesting experiment, and one in a series of changes in my career. Up until then, I'd just moved around all the time. But now, when Cleveland came along again, I was ready to settle down. I was tired of going from market to market, and I wanted to see if I could at least just live my life for a change.

Moving back to Cleveland turned out to be one of the best moves of my life.

Chapter Eight

Back to Cleveland— and the Radio Wars

WHEN I LEFT TAMPA to return to Cleveland in 1985, our whole business was going crazy. It was the era of the "radio wars." They were really nothing new, but they were about to be taken to a whole new level.

At my first stop in Denver, we didn't even have radio wars. We had promotions, but not open warfare with the competition. After that it was Colorado Springs and on to Albuquerque, and when I got there I tried to build a name for myself and get known. The big station in town was KOB and I was on KDEF. We were getting pretty well known, picking up ratings and getting better and better, but KOB was still the big station. We still had an effect.

At one point KOB said it was were bringing in a new morning man because of Lanigan, and he was from Cleveland. I can't remember his name and at that time I'd never been to Cleveland, but I'd heard about it from Joe Finan during my first stop in Denver. I was concerned. I thought, *Okay, I'm a goner. This guy's got to be good if he's from Cleveland. I'm probably through here.* But we held our own. What I most remember is feeling threatened because they were bringing in a guy from Cleveland. Cleveland was the big time.

When I first arrived in Cleveland in 1971, AM, was still king. I was at WGAR-AM and Mike Reineri at WIXY 1260 was probably our main competition. But he went to Miami after a few years, so it was me with the interviews and the craziness replacing Imus.

It's interesting because the people who were the competition when I first got there were Reineri and the guy who did "Chicken Man," Jim Runyon. He was there for a while and I was so impressed to meet him. There was never any anger or fights between the competition. Most people just wanted to do great radio. Remember Phil McLean? Wow, that guy had pipes. That voice started in the basement. The joke was that your dog never heard Phil McLean. His voice was that deep! Another great radio name, Ed Fisher, was there at the time. I was just a kid coming in against Reineri, Fisher, and Runyon, and I was honored to be there.

By 1972 WERE had its "People Power" format and Gary Dee was the competition. Years later, when I left Cleveland for Tampa, Gary's ex-wife, Liz Richards, was there, and a guy who was doing TV wanted to put us together on a mid-morning show, but we never worked it out. It would have meant cutting back on the radio show and I wasn't about to do that. But it would have been fun.

People Power! The stuff they put on the air. Can you imagine what kind of response it would get if it were new today, with social media? People today get upset over what you say, who you are, no matter what your opinion is. In a way, they were social media before it was invented.

Pete Franklin, the sports talk show host, was a force to be reckoned with, but he was on at night so he was no real competition for me. Then Gary Dee left WERE, where he was poorly promoted, for WHK-AM, and things got really crazy. Malrite owned WHK and WMMS and they were a promotion machine. Jeff and Flash at WMMS-FM would eventually be our other big competition.

In 1979 *Cleveland Magazine* had me on the cover choking Gary Dee. The cover story was an article by Dick Feagler titled: "The Morning Radio War for Ratings and Riches: Can John Lanigan (Or Anyone Else) Stop Gary Dee?"

We had totally different audiences. Overall we beat Dee in the ratings most of the time, but he obviously did very well too. His was more a talk show with callers, while ours was music with talk and guests.

By the mid-seventies, FM got serious and became a real player. But once Reineri was gone, Gary Dee was the guy I was mostly competing against. Jeff and Flash at WMMS eventually became competitors, but I never considered them real competition because I had a different audience with different demographics. Honestly, in those days demographics were just starting to be considered. It used to be that whatever the ratings were overall, 12+ was where you were. That's what I always went by, but then they started breaking it down to 18 to 25, 18 to 34, 18 to 49—those were the prime advertising groups. Radio began to change drastically, not so much for me but for the people I worked for, from the salesmen to the general manager. Jack Thayer was the general manager for a long time and I would see him arrive in the morning—sometimes 6 a.m.—and go straight back to his office to make calls all over the country.

Business is business but the real fun was still on the air. This was great radio. Dee and I attacked each other and made fun of each other but there was nothing malicious about it. We both left Cleveland at the same time. Dee was hired by the same two guys who hired me to go to Tampa, Norman Wain and Bob Weiss, and they sent him to Washington, D.C. They were just trying to help build up their properties, stations they owned outside of Cleveland. Plus, when they got rid of us, it helped their other stations in Cleveland because we were the competition. So they kind of fished in their own pond and decided what they wanted to do.

Gary Dee went to D.C. He made a lot of noise (including causing a firestorm with a joke about the wife of Mayor Marion Barry) but it didn't work and he ended up coming back to Cleveland just like me.

Before Dee's return and when I was in Tampa, I got a call from Morton Downey, Jr., who was making a career pit stop in Cleveland at WERE, replacing the late Count John Manolesco. He wanted us both to come on his show. We both agreed and did it from phones back in our studios. We had a good time joking about what we were doing, and I have to admit that I actually liked Gary Dee. When we were still in Cleveland we were competing at a really good level during the radio wars. Not like what I faced in Florida.

In Tampa I ran into an even more intense radio war. When I first arrived there the *Q Morning Zoo* was pretty much in control. It was the only time in my career that I could remember that there were four major morning shows competing against each other. Besides *Lanigan in the Morning* and the Q Zoo there was *London and Engleman*, who had come in from the west coast, and *Ron and Ron*, who were even more outrageous and over the top. They were on a rock station similar to WMMS. The four of us were battling back and forth and there was a lot of publicity about us.

Everybody did anything they could promotionally to get attention. That's why we did the boob-job campaign and the boat thing. We were trying some way to get the listeners to pay attention. There was a lot going on. Ron and Ron were very strong. They were like Jeff and Flash from WMMS in Cleveland. And the

Q Morning Zoo was one of the better-known radio shows in the country. They started the Morning Zoo format.

It was highly competitive time for a while, but it was amazing how in a year and a half all of those shows were gone. London and Engleman went back to the west coast, Ron and Ron broke up, I went back to Cleveland, and the Q Morning Zoo basically broke up too. Scott Shannon from the Zoo left for New York, where he was part of a different morning team at WHTZ that took over there. All are just memories.

I was always closer to management than programming, the people who were in charge of the radio station. Even the guy who fired me in Tampa. I went back to Cleveland, but the manager who fired me is one of my best drinking buddies in Tampa when I'm there. He'll call me on a Monday or Tuesday and say, "Meet me at the bar" and we get together all the time. His name is John Pinsch, and we get together because we're all over that. That's behind us.

Radio people are often very creative and don't like to be told what to do. I dealt with consultants and never really had a problem—most of the time. Mike McVay was a consultant but a good friend. Radio people are often insecure and McVay was one of the people I knew I could call if I needed a job. He was trying to get me back to Cleveland after I went to Tampa.

I had always wanted to work in New York and a morning job opened up there, at Malrite's WHTZ, "Z100." Their national program director had it down to two people for mornings in New York, me and Scott Shannon. I really wanted that job but didn't get it, so I was unhappy about that. Then when I got fired in Tampa I got flown to New York again for WOR-FM. The manager there really liked me and we went out to dinner that weekend.

"I think you could have fun here, I think it would work out," he said. "I liked you in Denver and Tampa and Cleveland." They got

The Political Boss Who Really Delivers
Those Costly Dieting Clinics: Are They Worth It?
Cleveland's Gays: Blending Into Society

AUGUST 1979 $1.50

CLEVELAND
MAGAZINE

**The Morning Radio War
For Ratings and Riches**

Can John Lanigan
(Or Anyone Else)
Stop Gary Dee?

Plus:
Bob August On Where
The Browns Went Wrong
And:
Pat Weitzel Reviews
Suburban Rib Joints

Courtesy of Cleveland Magazine

in touch with me, not me with them. That was after the manager
had fired me in Tampa because Norm Wain and Bob Weiss told
him to. The guy in New York told me, "Let's see if we can work
something out and get you here." He called this big-name consultant in St. Louis, and got back and said, "John, I want you but
the consultant doesn't like you! He doesn't think you're right for
the job."

Wait a minute! You're going to take some guy's opinion in St. Louis not to hire me in New York?

"I can't do it," he said "I have to go with the consultant. That's what he does."

Then I got the call to come home to the shores of Lake Erie.

I had wanted to come back to Cleveland and I talked to two stations, WMJI and another one. WMJI came up with a good deal. They said, "It's going to be fun. Go out here and do whatever you want." When I came back to Cleveland, changes had to be made. WMJI already had Kim and Dan doing the morning show, but they moved them to afternoons to make room for me. I felt bad about bumping two people off the morning show, but I needed a job, too.

The station changed with the morning show. It became more progressive with a new attitude, and got more current and in touch. More cutting edge.

The morning news person was John Webster, and after a while he became a big part of the show so it eventually became *Lanigan and Webster*. We also had other people on our team, like Tony Rizzo doing sports and David Moss doing entertainment stuff.

The competition might have underestimated me when I went to the FM dial. They might not have realized we were going after everybody. The station advertised me and promoted me and they did a lot of work. They paid me fairly well and the show started to gel. It was a good mix and the show took off. Webster was the news guy but we were looking for somebody to fill in for him once in a while because he was having health issues.

I was doing standup comedy at the Cleveland Comedy Club and one of the local guys there was really good. His name was Jimmy Malone and he became part of my radio show for many years. I think he could've been another Drew Carey or Steve Harvey, but he was a family guy and he didn't want to do the comedy-club circuit. He didn't want to live in his car like Carey had done for a time. Malone did this routine where one of the bits was "the funny news stories." We were doing a similar segment on our show called "Knuckleheads in the News," so I invited him to come on the show and include some of his bits. At least I think I did. To be honest, I didn't remember asking him.

One morning my staff said, "There's somebody in the lobby who's supposed to be on the show today." "Really? Who is it?' They said: "Jimmy Malone." Okay, I didn't remember asking him but I said, "Come on back," and the rest is history. He had this incredible laugh that was contagious and he played it for all it was worth. It became part of the show and eventually we started to use him more. Before long it became *Lanigan, Webster and Malone.* That might have been because of Malone's lawyer advising him to do that. "Knuckleheads" really took off. We even put out a couple "Best Of Knuckleheads" CDs that sold really well

First it was just Webster and me doing the "Knuckleheads," then it was the three of us, then Jimmy kind of took it over. He found the stories, which took some of the work off me. But after a time Webster was just not doing well and they didn't know what to do with him. Management made the decision that John was just not up to it anymore so they replaced him. (I enjoyed working with John, and I was saddened when he passed away just as this book was going to print.)

Chip Kullik was already working in the newsroom for the company, which by that time had four or five stations. So when Webster left, Kullik moved in. He was the news guy, but after the news he'd sit in with us and he became part of the show as well. He was younger and pepped things up a bit.

Along the way we decided we needed a female voice and somebody to take care of the guests. We had a lot of guests on the show and we needed someone to book interviews and get them orga-

My partner John Webster and me on a large WMJI billboard along the West Shoreway overlooking Municipal Stadium.

nized. Somehow we found Tracy Carrol, who had been working in Akron and was looking to get into Cleveland. Malone and I met her for lunch, we clicked and she became part of it, too. We were ready for the radio wars of the 1990s.

WMMS-FM was still our main morning competition. They were the *Buzzard Morning Zoo* and they were playing hardball. Sometimes they would call up the guests that we had coming on. We'd be promoting them all week and then they'd call them and pretend to be us. They would tell them, "I'm sorry but we're not going to be able to use you today. Lanigan's really booked solid so we'll have to forget the interview."

It really got crazy. And dirty. I think one time they even left a dead animal on my doorstep. Today John Gorman, their program director back then, is one of my best friends. But that's what the radio wars were all about. They were really fun—and sometimes messy.

WMMS took it personally when they went after you. I had just come back in 1987 when they went after me.

WMMS was leading the way to bring the Rock and Roll Hall of Fame to Cleveland. They were trying to take all the credit for the campaign, but I went after them and the Rock Hall. They tried to make it look like I was against the Hall coming to Cleveland, which I really wasn't. I was delighted about the project. A lot of people deserved credit for it, not just WMMS. They were like the giant gorilla in the room that you just couldn't ignore.

WMMS was lambasting me, claiming that I was anti-rock and roll. We were an oldies channel, so we didn't consider ourselves as rock and roll as they did. They were hard rock and they did a great job. Kid Leo was a radio god and they brought huge acts through town like Bruce Springsteen, John Mellencamp, Bon Jovi and on and on, and they all came through WMMS.

It was a really competitive time and a lot of fun but let me stress, it was a war.

It took a really nasty turn when Howard Stern came to town. He was nationally syndicated but was on in Cleveland at WNCX. Stern had already used sleazy personal stuff to wipe out the competition in Philadelphia and Rochester, New York. My bosses told me Howard was being syndicated around the country and we were the next city on the list.

I remember one manager stressing to me that he wanted me to be prepared. I said I knew that he was a big deal in New York but I wasn't really worried about him. That didn't ease his fears a bit.

"John, it's not the same thing that you've fought before," he said. "This is something different. He's not going to be nice."

"Oh, not a problem," I replied. But I had no idea how bad it would get.

Singer Petula Clark joined our morning show crew at WMJI's downtown studio on West Sixth and Lakeside. Her signature song was "Downtown." (Left to right) Me, John Webster, Clark, and Jimmy Malone. Circa 1989.

Radio became vicious. Stern got nasty and dirty, and attacking my wife, my station and everything about me. He was much dirtier than WMMS ever was.

Maybe other stations did , but I never underestimated Stern. Years before, when I was in Florida and Stern had left the radio station in Washington, D.C., they tried to get me to go to that station. One of the guys there was from Florida, he called and asked if I was interested, but I said no. I had been through it once before, replacing Imus, and I didn't want to go through that again, being the guy who would replace Stern. Thanks, but no thanks.

Stern was a whole different animal. He liked to attack his competition.

He went after a DJ in Philadelphia, John DeBella. DeBella was a big deal, and Stern went after him big time to take him down. Anything he could find to embarrass him, he used. He had DeBella's ex-wife on the air, and he goaded her into badmouthing DeBella, very personally. She was later found dead in her garage with her car engine running. The coroner called it suicide.

I don't know how you live with that kind of radio. If you think that's entertaining, I don't agree with you.

In Cleveland, Stern went after Jeff and Flash first, and they went down in flames fast. WMMS management told them, "Don't respond. Whatever he does, you stay out of it, don't respond." They didn't, and Stern was wiping the dust off his hands within a few months. That was the wrong way to try to handle Stern. You can't just go and take the beatings and not say anything back. He was yelling and screaming things about everyone, just going after people.

Then he turned on me.

I didn't really care. What could he do to me?

We had a special telephone at our station that we called the "hot line." It was an emergency line for people who needed to get hold of someone inside the station and for company business only. It was not a line that anyone outside is supposed to know about. Potential guests would use it so we could set it up to talk to them on the air, but other than that, the number was strictly confidential. It wasn't confidential for long after Stern went on the air.

One day I picked up the line after I was off the air and it was Stern yelling at me. Somebody had sold out and given him that number, somebody who worked at our station. That really pissed me off.

He started going after me on the air.

But then he started going after my wife. He was making fun of her, saying she was a Playboy bunny and that she must be blind to marry a loser like me. He claimed she was stuck in Cleveland with me and my dog and so on and so on. Plus, he promised a huge personal appearance in Cleveland if he ever reached number one, as he'd done in other cities. He called these appearances funerals, and the numbers were lining up for him in Cleveland really quick. Word got out that Stern's next "funeral" would be in the Flats.

Usually Sandy didn't listen to him, but one day she came home with tears running down her face. She said, "I don't know what's going on. I'm not in radio. I don't have anything to do with this." Then we started getting calls from our friends on the west coast, from people who listened to him, because he was syndicated out there, too. They were saying, "Man, he's really after you now, isn't he?" It really hurt Sandy and I wasn't sure what to do. Then one day I got a call from a Cleveland cop who said, "Do you want to talk for a minute after the show?" Sure!

"I'm not really crazy about you but I really don't like Howard Stern," the cop said. "He's just an absolutely disgusting human being." OK, but what's your point? He told me, "If you want something to fight back against him with, let me give you some facts."

He gave me a whole pile of dirt about the people working at WNCX, from the owners to the on-air personalities. He claimed a jock there was a prostitute, another was wanted by Interpol, there had been drug busts, one of the owners' family members had been arrested . . .

"I thought you might be able to use it," the cop said, "because Howard doesn't seem to care what he uses."

I thanked him.

A few days after that I came home and Sandy was crying again about Howard's comments. *This is where it stops*, I thought. At that point I was absolutely livid! *When you attack my family, you piece of shit, I'm going to come back.* I was driving to WUAB for the *Prize Movie* and I picked up the phone and called the owners of

WNCX, Norm Wain and Bob Weiss, the same guys who had hired and fired me in Florida. Weiss picked up the phone and said, "Hi John, how you doing? How's everything going?"

"You piece of shit!" I yelled. "I am so sick of this. Would you like to have your wife attacked like that?! Howard Stern is tearing my wife apart and she doesn't have anything to do with this business, and if he doesn't stop there's going to be hell to pay!"

"Well, I can't tell Howard to stop," Weiss said. "He's in New York and he doesn't pay any attention to us. It's a syndicated show."

I'm not buying it.

"I heard about some of the crap he pulled in Philly and Rochester," I said. "I'll tell you what I'm going to do. If you can't stop him, I'm going to have a press conference of my own in the Flats, when he's here for his little get-together. When he comes in to belittle us all and show how big he is, I'm going to have a press conference at the same time. And I'm going to tell the people about your station."

Then I proceeded to tell him all the dirt the Cleveland cop told me. Dead silence on his end. Then Weiss started stuttering, "John, John, John—" I had heard enough, and I cut him off.

"You know what? Screw you Bob," I said. "I don't give a damn what you think. You think people won't come if I do a press conference of my own during this whole Flats thing? I guarantee you it'll be covered just like Howard will."

"Don't do anything," Weiss said, sounding nervous "Let me talk to Norm. He's not here right now." I told him I didn't care, and it was obvious I was really upset. Despite Florida, Bob and I had been very civil with each other in the past. Not now. I was just livid.

Weiss pleaded, "Thank you, but please don't do anything."

I was as cordial as I could be. "Screw you," I said, and hung up.

I did the *Prize Movie*, and when I got home the phone rang. It was the owner of my station, Carl Hirsch, who lived in California. The first words out of his mouth were, "What have you done?"

"What do you mean?" I asked. But I knew, and I told him about my call to Weiss. Hirsch warned it was about to get ugly. Real ugly.

"Here's what's going to happen," he said. "The owners are very upset with you. This time Norman is going to call you and he's going to try to get you to talk to him like you did to Bob. Threaten him. Then they're going to sue you for trying to threaten them."

Huh? Sue *me*?

"That's pretty much the way I understand it. Just be careful how you talk to him."

An hour later the phone rang, and sure enough, it was Norm Wain.

"Hi John, how are you? I need to talk to you about this conversation that you had with Bob. What you're going to do?"

I wasn't about to hold back.

"Your morning guy is making fun of my wife and I don't understand any of that," I said.

"Well John, you know we can't control Howard."

I said that's fine, but I have to fight back and do what I can. When he asked what I planned to do, I just told him, "Wait and see."

We talked for a few minutes but he couldn't get me upset and I didn't call him any names. I kept Hirsch's warning in mind. Wain knew what was going on, too. He basically said that there was nothing he could do with Stern and that he hated what I was going to do but he guessed that I had to do what I had to do. I left him with this:

"You guys were great to work for and I'm sorry about all this, but what Howard's been doing is just not right. There's no reason to put up with his crap. Just keep that in mind."

I later heard that they had called Stern out of a meeting in New

York and told him that he had to leave Lanigan's wife alone. But this was Howard Stern. Word is, he said, "Go screw yourself. I'll do what I want!" and left the room. Stern didn't listen to anybody, and with his ratings he didn't have to. As it turned out, though, Howard never mentioned my wife again. He came at me numerous times, but he never said anything about Sandy again. I never had the press conference.

I didn't care about the so-called Stern "funeral" in the Flats. I was on the air when it was going on and all the attention then went to the guy from WMMS who cut the wires and took WNCX off the air. I might have seen some of it on TV that night, but they were focusing on the engineer and his wire cutters. Keep in mind that the funeral was in June 1994 and our parent company, OmniAmerica, had taken over WMMS a couple of months before. Jeff and Flash were no longer the morning team at 'MMS, and we were now sister stations, still with two distinct audiences.

The Lanigan–Stern battle continued back and forth until he left for Sirius XM radio. Later I had comedians come on our show who had also been on his show and they would say they were talking to Stern about me. And he would say he didn't quite understand me and how I did it but he didn't talk about Sandy again.

And Stern never beat me 12+. Not once. In other demographics at times he did, but never 12+.

Radio might have hardened me up a bit. The business certainly made you pay close attention to what was going on. But I didn't hold a grudge against Wain and Weiss. Stern didn't really work for them, he was just on their channel. Later Wain even called me and asked if his son could come on our show. David Wain is a really successful producer in Hollywood, and had a movie coming out, so I said, "Sure, of course. I'd love to have him on." They came up to do the show that morning and Norm Wain kind of hung in the back of the room, like he didn't know what I was going to say to him. I went over and shook his hand and said: "It's nice to see you. Sorry about all the problems we had, but it's good to have you here."

The Buzzard Morning Zoo had a head start on me on the FM dial, but they eventually fell by the wayside and Stern was a major reason. I obviously didn't think much of Howard Stern. He had a good act but it was at a lot of people's expense. I thought Don Imus was interesting and was talented. But I didn't like Jeff Kinzbach. Flash is a good guy and I've talked to him a number of times since. I tried to say hi to them both when I came back from Florida at one of the auto races held at Burke Lakefront Airport. I saw them, walked over, and said, "Hi guys!" Jeff looked at me and said, "Screw you!" and walked away. Flash didn't say much, just gave me a disgusted look. I've talked to Flash many times since and done promotional stuff with him and I like the guy a lot. There might have been a little bit of a problem about money, what I was making and what they were making.

Eventually, the other guys were long gone from Cleveland's morning airwaves. But I was still there.

Chapter Nine

For the Love of Cleveland

THERE ARE QUITE A few things that I was involved in during my long career in Cleveland that I have to admit I'm kind of proud of. Some of them were on the air and some of them off. One is the Bob Feller statue at Progressive Field. It all started with a simple dinner in Bay Village.

I became friends with Feller though Rocco Scotti. They're both gone now, but Scotti was a good friend and was famous for singing the "Star Spangled Banner" at Indians games. He had a great voice and I had him on the show a lot.

He was also a good friend of Bob Feller's. It turns out Feller and I shared a birthday, November 3. If Feller was in town on that date, we'd all go out to dinner, including Scotti and our wives. We did that for a number of years, usually at a restaurant in Little Italy that Feller really loved. But then one year we decided to meet on the west side, since Scotti and I lived in that part of town. It was in Bay Village, in a little Chinese restaurant in a small strip mall that's no longer there.

So the six of us were talking and joking and at one point someone said something about statues that were being built at some stadium. I don't know who brought it up but someone said to Feller, "How come there's not one of you? Look at you. You're Bob Feller, for god's sake."

"I like that idea!" he said. "Let's get me a statue." Scotti wondered how to get the campaign under way and Feller mentioned, "Well, you got a radio show. Why don't you do something about it?" We all agreed that was a great idea, and in just days we started talking about it on the air.

It seemed like a no-brainer. "Wouldn't it be great if the Indians had a statue of Bob Feller?" I said. "Here's one of the greatest ballplayers of all time and he's got nothing. Other cities have statues of some of their players outside their stadiums." We talked it up and found a sculptor, and the ball really started rolling. Now don't get me wrong, the Indians held the power to get this done, but everyone was really quite into it.

Eventually it was taken away from us, but we put the idea out there. After the unveiling it became the focal point of the new stadium. People would say all the time, "I'll meet you at the Bob Feller statue."

There have been others, including Jim Thome, but Feller was the first. If you wanted to have a brick around it with your name on it, you could pay so much and be part of the project. The Indians gave me and Scotti bricks right next to Feller's statue for coming up with the idea. Kind of a thank you, or whatever. Let me also point out that not everything was smooth sailing with this project.

Feller didn't like how his leg came out. They had to work on it a little bit to get the balance right so that it looked like Feller when he was pitching, but it all worked out in the end. It all started at a Chinese restaurant in Bay Village. I'm not the biggest baseball fan in the world, but I've always been happy about that.

Another incident that stands out in my mind was when we were broadcasting on September 11, 2001. It was pretty much a normal morning until Chip Kullik, our news guy, came in and said he had a story from New York City that a plane had just flown into the World Trade Center. I can still remember vividly the first time we checked and saw the smoke pouring out of the World Trade Center. At our studio in Independence we had a TV in the upper corner, just off to my right side.

At first we laughed about it, thinking how bad of a pilot could you be that you couldn't miss the World Trade Center, for god's sake? I mean, those towers are huge. How could someone just fly into it?

The first report was that it was a small plane, so we thought it had to be a pilot who had a heart attack or somehow became incapacitated. But as we kept watching, we saw the second plane fly into the second building, and things got really serious. At that point a lot of people thought we might actually be in a war.

We stayed on the air, talking about what was going on. Mark "Munch" Bishop, our sports guy, was on the show and said that he had a friend in New York City who worked close to the WTC. We called him and he was in his office where he could see the World Trade Center. He said, yes, two planes had flown into it and it was a nightmare. It seemed like there were people dying everywhere.

By that time we had found out that it wasn't a small plane as we had first thought, but passenger jets. There were a lot of people who were dead and with all the news coverage that was going on, we just stayed on the air live with Munch's friend.

Our show normally ended at 10, but we stayed on until almost noon. We were basically there for the people who weren't close to a TV. We described everything we saw, but we also had Munch's friend in New York, who was a big plus. He described the nightmare that was happening as people jumped out of the windows to their deaths.

There was a report that a plane had been diverted at Cleveland Hopkins Airport, that it turned around here and was headed back

The WMJI morning show teamed up with radio station WZAK for a kids' clothing drive on the steps of Cleveland City Hall. Cars would pull up to the curb and drop off clothes. I'm in the middle with Cleveland Mayor George Voinovich, wearing a white rain coat. WZAK radio personality Lynn Tolliver on my left. *(City of Cleveland)*

toward Washington, D.C. Every plane had been ordered out of the air and they all landed, so there was absolutely nothing in the air but that plane. It came here and turned around and headed back over Pennsylvania, where it finally went down in the field. But it was heading back to Washington to try and hit the White House. We were also getting reports that it might be headed our way; that maybe it was going to fly into something in Cleveland.

We stayed on, and any info that we could get was put right on the show. We just opened the lines up so people could talk about it and then we kept them informed as best we could. I've talked to people who years later would stop me and say, "I've got to thank you for that because I couldn't get to anything to watch it. I had you guys on the whole time and you guys described it so vividly to us that we felt like we were there."

I'm kneeling with the trophy we won in a charity race against the Cleveland Browns team at the Cleveland Metroparks toboggan chute in Strongsville. We beat coach Bill Belichick's team the first time, but he made us race a second time—and he loaded up his team with some of the biggest Browns players I'd ever seen, to go even faster. He did not like to lose.

The guy in New York just made a world of difference. He was able to tell us what it looked like, with the people and the dust and the whole mess that was coming down from up there. No one appreciated how bad it looked around the World Trade Center.

That was a day I'll never forget. None of us will.

There was another day in the studio that stands out in my mind as well. The AIDS scare was just beginning and we invited a guy with the disease into the studio.

At the time, AIDS was getting wide media coverage, but there was a lot of bad information out there. We did our research and we knew for a fact from talking to doctors that it couldn't be transmitted by somebody just breathing on you. That's not how

HIV was passed on, but it was still something that a lot of people believed.

So we invited a guy with AIDS to come on our show and talk about what it was like and what he was going through. The guys in the studio were cool with it, but other people at the station, like the sales staff, didn't come in that day. They thought what we were doing was a bad idea and didn't want to get exposed to it. We tried to tell them that you can't get AIDS by talking to someone about it. The overall response was, "It doesn't matter. We don't believe that. We're not coming in."

The panic about HIV and AIDS was unbelievable. But people were suffering from the disease and we just decided to have the AIDS victim on to talk about it and to try to clear up some of the misunderstandings. We thought that was a good thing to do but we were totally surprised by some of the reactions we got, and I'm glad we did it.

Some days stay with you, like when the space shuttle Challenger blew up. We weren't on the air when it happened, but everyone remembers where they were when they first heard about it. I saw it at home when I was living in Lakewood at the time, and when I went to the station the next day we decided to stop doing any comedy material for a while. We still did interviews, but we stayed away from making any jokes. It just didn't feel right. Nothing was funny. So we suspended our regular programming for about three days. It was just the right thing to do.

Sometimes ratings take a back seat.

We once did a simulcast with WZAK, the top-rated black radio station in town, to collect clothes for poor kids. We were there with Lynn Tolliver and Ralph Poole, their morning show hosts, on the steps of Cleveland's city hall. People drove by and dropped off clothes as they went to work. Tolliver's show staff and our folks worked together to gather up the donations, and it was a real successful outing on both sides. Mayor Voinovich even stopped by for a bit to join us. I always enjoyed working with Tolliver and his staff. It was kind of unusual for two stations to team up like that, but we were just trying to do some good. I think it worked out pretty well.

One of the best things that ever happened to me was when I made the cover of *Cleveland Magazine* in December 2002. That year they had a story about the thirty most important people in Cleveland from the previous thirty years. When I saw the cover and I was one of them, I said, "You know what? That's as good as it gets."

They put me along with legends like Dorothy Fuldheim and Bernie Kosar and so many other people who were part of Cleveland. For them to consider me one of the thirty most important people in the city for that period of time was one of the best things that had ever happened to me. It meant that I was part of this big city that I didn't even come from. I didn't live there my whole life but I had spent enough time there that they thought I was one of the most important things in the city. Trust me, Cleveland is really important to me, too.

Chapter Ten

Part-Time Gigs

MY RADIO CAREER WAS always my main source of income, but I often tried my hand at other jobs. Most of them were offshoots of my radio show. Over the years I dabbled in television, worked as a disc jockey, emceed many events and tried my hand as a standup comic. This goes back to when I was in high school in Nebraska. I got my start as an emcee, playing records at sock hops in the school gym. I wasn't really doing any material. I just emceed what was going on, and I was working at the local radio station in the afternoon. I got used to working two shifts a day at an early age. That was an easy gig for a radio guy, because I got to meet a lot of famous people for at least a few minutes backstage when I was introducing them.

I once opened for a Bob Hope fundraiser in Akron. Hope was backstage with his wife and even the family dog. He followed a couple other acts, and when I finally went out to introduce Hope, the dog got away from his wife. It ran the whole length of the backstage area, right through everything, knocking things over and then right through the big curtains. Once it got to the front of the stage it ran right up to Hope. I was in the process of introducing him when we saw the dog coming at us, and it really wanted his attention. Hope looked at me, then looked at the dog and just swooped it up. He lifted it up in the air, hugged it for a minute to huge applause and then handed it over to me. He didn't miss a beat.

"I'll take over now, okay?" he said.

I gave the dog to his wife, Dolores, who was standing offstage. That was Bob Hope, the professional. I did get a chance to talk to Hope and his wife backstage and told him that my mother, Betty Lanigan, was a huge fan of his. His wife said, "My god, Betty Lanigan? There was a Betty Lanigan who worked for us. She was one of our PR people who handled our stuff in L.A." It wasn't my mom, of course. I'd heard that story once before and I wasn't sure if it was true or not so I kind of dropped her name. My mom really got a kick out of that story when I told her. Bob Hope was always one of my favorites because he was such a nice guy and everybody loved that he was from Cleveland. He was just a personable guy and his wife was a delight.

I did lots of work in the Akron-Canton area. They'd have big New Year's Eve parties and they'd hire me to host them. We had a team that went with us. I had a gal I hired who had a sound system that she brought in with a partner. Anywhere that I was booked, they were booked along with me. They'd set up the microphones and speakers, we'd do our show and I'd emcee the rest of the show with all the acts and silly contests to get people out of the audience and up on their feet. I did that gig for years, and it was a good way to make money. People paid more because it was New Year's Eve. We'd pick up over a thousand dollars for that evening instead of the two or three hundred bucks on a regular night. So instead of celebrating New Year's Eve with my family, we'd go on a nice vacation the week after. The people down in Akron were terrific, a great audience.

I had a regular standup routine for about ten or fifteen minutes.

It was a set format and it didn't vary a lot except maybe I'd try out new games once in a while, silly games like Jimmie Fallon does now on *The Tonight Show*. Which brings me to my short and sweet standup comic career. It was another dream of mine that never quite materialized.

When I first came to Cleveland, there was something called The Cleveland Comedy Club. It was located where Progressive Field is today. The early comedy clubs were where all these young comics were just starting out. I was trying to jump start my standup career back then, too, so I got to meet a lot of the comics who came through there. They were absolutely the best and most of them are still working today in that upper echelon of comedy. The club had everybody, guys like Jerry Seinfeld, Steve Harvey and Drew Carey. They were there all the time. I'd watch these guys and they were all really good. They'd travel all over the country. I'd meet the comics at the club and then invite them to be guests on my morning radio show. We got into using comics on the show all the time. Instant guest list!

A lot of them are still doing it, like Bob Saget, who I got to know pretty well. Saget was hilarious, but he was as dirty as hell. People who knew him from his *Full House* TV show, playing a caring dad, would go see the show and walk away stunned. That sure wasn't what they expected, but Bobby was great.

I also got to know Saget's co-star from *Full House*, comedian Dave Coulier. We did a lot of remotes, and this one time he was our guest when we did our radio show from the window of Higbee's downtown in the Terminal Tower. We figured that people could come down and meet him. That was when *Full House* was doing really well. I've met Coulier a number of times since then, and he always brings up that time in the window and what a good time he had.

The way the Comedy Club was set up, you could basically walk across the stage and go right to a table. One night Bill Kirchenbauer was on and somebody was heckling him real badly. So he walked over to the guy's table and shouted, "Shut the hell up!" Then they all marched out and went at it in the parking lot. It was a great comedy club. They don't exist like that anymore.

I was trying to hone my own standup act for a while. I did a forty-minute show but it just didn't make it. I realized that it wasn't what I wanted to do. I just wasn't that good and I was watching the best, like Jerry Seinfeld, and all the rest of them. That's pretty much what cured me of that dream.

A lot of great local comics came out of there. Look at Steve Harvey. He was around all the time, and he's huge now. He's one of the busiest guys in show business. He has his own radio show and his own TV show and he's got all kinds of other things going on. He's a good guy and we had him on our radio show a lot. But it takes a whole lot of work to really make it. Look at Drew Carey. He went from Cleveland to national TV but he lived in his car for a while. It was a tough road but they all stuck with it and they made it pay off big-time.

Another comic I met in Cleveland was John Pinette. One morning during my radio show, I looked out in the lobby and there was this big, heavy-set guy in a t-shirt and jeans sitting out there. He was really overweight. Technically he would be called morbidly obese. I asked, "Who the hell is that?" Our producer said he was this guy from the Comedy Club and he's on next. Well, he came in and just destroyed us. It was one of the funniest sets I'd ever seen, and every time he came back to town he always did the show and he always killed us. Pinette was doing cruise ships and traveling all over the country. He was even in the final episodes of *Seinfeld*, but he wasn't doing well health-wise. Then one day somebody called me and said: "He died last night." It was a tragedy, because he was really funny.

I tried my hand at television, too. It went back to the great time I had as TV weatherman in New Mexico. For a while I was an entertainment reporter on Channel 3 for the 6 o'clock news program. It was just once a week on Thursdays, and I'd sit at the news desk and the anchor would ask me what was going on around town for the weekend. Then we'd show this stuff we'd recorded out on location. I did it for a little while but I didn't really like it very much so I left it behind. It was too much work, having to go out and record stuff, then go back downtown every day. It became a drag so I gave it to the guy who was working with me and he took it over.

I had another short TV gig as *Lanigan at Large*. It was a Sunday night show and WUAB sent me all over the country to interview film stars just before their movies were coming out. It was kind of like what David Moss does today. It was fun but that got old, too, so that's another one I gave up.

That was pretty much my television career except for the *Prize Movie*, which we've already discussed, but there was one other simulcast experiment that Channel 61 tried with my radio show.

It was back in the early days when we were still *Lanigan and Webster*. Channel 61 was an early cable channel, like Channel 43. They were already trying these simulcasts in several other markets. Don Imus was doing the same thing in New York on a cable channel. So they put cameras in our radio studio and broadcast us live on television as we did our show. It was a big deal at the time and we did it for about a year, but I don't know if it ever worked all that well.

It's tough doing a show like that. We kept in mind that there was a camera on us at all times. It became the Channel 61 *Lanigan and Webster in the Morning Show* simulcast, and I think it was on that station because they didn't have much else in the form of morning programming. Guests would come on, and I guess the

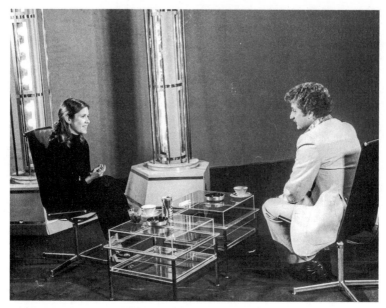

Interviewing Carrie Fischer when I visited the set of *Star Wars* in 1977. I had just finished interviewing Harrison Ford, and I told Carrie what a quiet, low-key guy he was. Carrie said, "Yeah, yeah, that gets him so many girls." Ford was working as a carpenter at the time.

viewers did like to see what the guests looked like. But we had to play video along with music and there were issues with AFTRA, the broadcast union. Some announcers who did radio spots demanded the additional pay for TV voiceovers.

Even though I gave up television and standup I continued to do emcee work, and I dabbled in nightclubs because I had one named after me. It was called Lanigan's, although I didn't own it. It was the brainchild of Hank LoConti, the owner of the Agora concert venue, and it was run by an Agora alumnus, Buddy Maver. LoConti knew me from when I'd emceed events at the Agora such as the air guitar contests on Sunday nights.

One day he said, "Let's open up a Lanigan's. I've got a place where I want to put a club in and if you don't mind we'll use your

Another *Lanigan at Large* interview, with Clint Eastwood on the ranch used for the set of the movie *The Outlaw Josie Wales* in Santa Fe, New Mexico. Circa 1976.

name and make it that. You only have to come out there once or twice a week." It was the old Celebrity Room hall at Mayfield and SOM Center Roads. When he suggested that, I thought, *I've got to go along with this guy. He's a genius.* He really was. The Agora had to be one of the best nightclubs in America for many years. Everybody played there.

"Okay I'll try it," I said, but it never really took off. It was in the Eastgate Shopping Mall. That's where Saints and Sinners had been, and that was a great club. They had all kinds of huge names, like Ricky Nelson, appear there, but the club had closed and gone away. We opened Lanigan's in the same shopping center but not the same location. We couldn't duplicate its success, and I'm not sure why. LoConti tried everything to make it work, but it just didn't make any money. We even had a lot of great acts come through there, like the Mamas and the Papas. Eric Carmen of the Raspberries stopped by a lot and I even got the chance to sing on stage with him, but it just never came together all that well. To LoConti's credit, even though it was losing money, he made sure that nobody got burned. Everybody got paid all the way around. LoConti was as standup a guy as you'll ever meet. He would continue his success at the Agora and even other countries.

After Lanigan's, I decided that was it for me. I wasn't going to get involved in anything like that again. When I was young I didn't mind staying up late at the nightclub and waking up early for my radio show, but it got a lot harder when I got older. So that was it for my nightclub career.

Chapter Eleven

What If?

As I look back on a long radio career, I have to admit that in my early days my dream was to make it to the big time, markets like New York or L.A. I did have a few close calls but I never quite made it. The funny thing is that my first chance to go to New York wasn't even on the radio. It was on the stage. My interest in acting went all the way back to my high school days. I played Ali Hakim in *Oklahoma* when I was in high school. He was the only one in the entire show who did not sing, so that role was made for me.

I had fun and I got the acting bug. So when I was working in New Mexico in the late 1960s, I got to know Bernie Thomas, who was the director of the Albuquerque Little Theatre. He put these incredible productions together that were really well attended. He had a great theater and a great group of people who worked there. He brought in lots of top-name people from Hollywood like Don Knotts from *The Andy Griffith Show* and Vivian Vance from *I Love Lucy*.

I was fortunate to be cast in three plays, but it was kind of tough because I was doing my radio show in the morning and my TV weatherman gig on the early and late evening news. So I had to give up my early evening TV show to work the theater. Vivian

Vance did a play with us called *Everybody's Girl*. At the time she was living in Santa Fe with her husband and was a huge star from the *Lucy* show. She would always bring in pizza for all of us backstage. She was a delightful woman who was always accommodating for everyone.

Our director was John Patrick, who had won a Pulitzer Prize for writing the play *Tea House of the August Moon*, and the Pulitzer made him a major player. All the pieces fell into place.

The play drew sell-out crowds in Albuquerque, and Patrick wanted to take it to New York. He had plans to stage it off-Broadway to see if it worked, and said, "Why don't you come with us, John, and try it out?"

"I'd like to," I said, "but I have a family here and kids and a radio show and a TV show and as much as I'd love to do this—and you have no idea how much—I can't do it. Thanks."

Patrick took it to New York without me and it only ran for three weeks before it closed. But I always wondered what it would have been like to be on the stage in New York City. I really wanted to work with John Patrick. You don't get many chances to work with somebody like that and have a chance to go to New York. If I hadn't been married, if it hadn't been a big deal, maybe I could've just taken off and gone to the Big Apple. But I wasn't done just yet.

When I came to Cleveland I kept dabbling in the theater. I did plays in Bay Village and Lakewood and North Royalton, but I never had a major opportunity like that again. Patrick came to Cleveland once to do a play in Berea and I got to talk with him again. He was always a delightful person.

There was another time years before when I had a chance to go to Los Angeles, but I didn't take that opportunity either. My friend Mark Blinoff was the program director at KMPC, which was one of L.A.'s big pop music channels at the time. He called me when I was working in Denver and said, "I need somebody to work the all-night shift." But I'd always been a morning man, so I said I didn't want to do it, even though I really wanted to go to L.A. and work in Hollywood. I turned it down, so he hired Sonny Melendrez from San Antonio. He stayed there for years. I talked to him on and off for a while during that time and he finally quit and went back to San Antonio. Melendrez told me, "You know, John, I just never saw myself getting off the all-night show there and working up to another daytime slot."

I would have been in the same spot. None of the people working there ever left. Guys like Dick Whittington and Gary Owens and Jim Lange, legendary voices that were part of KMPC, stayed there forever. So Melendrez left and went back to San Antonio until he retired a while back. That was another "what if?" It would have been fun to go to L.A. and do voiceovers at Disney like Melendrez did, but he never got off the all-night show. So you never know. I kind of thought it was just like Broadway. I just couldn't do it at the time. There were too many other people who expected me to be there for them.

I had another close call with Hollywood fame, but this one came in Cleveland.

Back in 1979, Gene Norris approached me about hosting a TV pilot. He was a local promoter for the Miss Cleveland contest and publisher of a newspaper called *Nightlife*. The pilot was called *The Divorce Game*. *The Newlywed Game* was really popular back then and the rules were the same. I was the emcee who asked questions and the men tried to predict how the women would answer and the women tried to do the same. We were trying to generate conflict.

Here's the problem: We tried to get the divorced people to fight over basic things like money or whatever. I believe it was just too touchy at the time. I think it would work today, quite frankly, because anything goes anymore. We did a half-hour show with a bunch of divorced people fighting back and forth to try to win prizes.

We filmed the pilot at Channel 43's studio, the same place where we did the *Prize Movie*. It was an interesting game show and it didn't get as tense as we thought it would. We thought there could be some really bad feelings between people going through it. I'm sure if they did it long-term it might have been that way, but we only did one episode.

Norris took it to some people in Hollywood, the same people who did the *Newlywed Game*, to see if they'd be interested. They shopped it around and there was a little interest in it but everybody just decided it was too touchy. They all said the same thing: "It's just not now. I don't think the country's ready for this."

He came back and told me, "John, nobody wants to pick it up. They don't want to take a chance on it. It's a little too outrageous for them." There went my chance to be another Drew Carey or Steve Harvey.

My last chance to go to New York City was when I working in television, doing entertainment news for Channel 3. One time I was interviewing Tony Bennett. He was doing a concert in Cleveland so I helped promote it.

We had the camera crew with us and we did some really fun interviews with him. We did it a couple of times and Bennett said, "This is great. I love working with you. You ought to be in New York."

"Yeah, yeah, yeah," I said, "from your mouth to God's ear."

"No, I mean it," he said. "You really should come to New York. Just get me a tape of this interview. I want a tape that I can take back with me." I didn't have a tape but he gave me an address and told me to get one to him pronto. So I went home and I thought, no, I'm not going to bother him with that. It's ridiculous.

And then I thought, well, what if something came out of it?

I sent it and then I got it back in the mail a few days later, with a note from his son, who handled all of his business stuff: "My dad is not in the business of getting people jobs," or something to that effect, "but thank you for your interest." Huh?

I just let it go. Maybe I shouldn't have bothered sending a tape, but after all, it was Tony who had said over and over again, "Send me a tape. I want a tape." Okay, his son was his manager, and I can understand his reaction. Tony was a legend. Too bad we couldn't have worked together in the Big Apple.

Chapter Twelve

Let's Get the Show on the Road

THE MORNING SHOW ON WMJI didn't always stay in the studio. It was fun to do remotes and that also meant a lot of fresh new guests. An old friend from Cleveland is Sherrod Brown, now U.S. Senator Sherrod Brown. I knew him from way back, when he lost the Ohio Secretary of State race in 1990. It wasn't a good time for Brown. He was pretty down and out and was considering giving up on politics. He even thought about a career in radio. Brown asked me, "Do you think that's a possibility?"

I didn't think it was a good idea and told him so.

"Don't give up," I said, "go back and do it again. You're going to be okay." Brown wasn't convinced, but he went back and ran for Congress and won and before you knew it, he was in the Senate. He always remembered my advice, and offered some good ideas of his own.

It was his idea for a program out of D.C. that really set us apart from the competition. We were having dinner one time in the early 1990s and he said: "You ought to come to Washington and do the show." That idea appealed to me immediately, but we had to go back and sell it to the station. There was a cost involved because we took several people with us, like my co-hosts, Chip

Kullik, Jimmie Malone, and Tracey Carroll. At different times we brought different people, but we had to feed them and put them in hotel rooms. That cost the station money and the shows really didn't bring in any extra revenue for them because they weren't sponsored. But it worked, and everyone in town talked about those shows and we enjoyed them immensely.

Word got around about the broadcasts from Capitol Hill and it wasn't long before other politicians were lining up for some free air time. We expanded our stay to have a day with Congressman Brown and then maybe a day with Ohio Senator Mike DeWine. Then Ohio's other senator, George Voinovich, said: "Why are you leaving me out? Why don't you do a show with me?"

Of course we did. It was a great fun, and had lots of great guests.

A lot of times Sherrod would help me book the show. He would call me and say, "I got somebody for you." And it wasn't just politicians. Sometimes Sherrod lined us up with other interesting people, like the congressional barber. He was the barber in the Capitol building and gave haircuts to all of the movers and shakers. We had a chance to find out who was difficult to give haircuts to and who wasn't, and whom he liked and didn't like.

We even interviewed one of the drivers who took all the congressmen to their various events. Sherrod liked to find people who were working in the Capitol and bring them along. It was great fun, but what was really interesting was how many of the senators we interviewed later ran for President. There was one time Sherrod called me and said, "You need to talk to this guy; he's great. You're going to like him but he's a little bit off the norm." It was Bernie Sanders.

Bernie was just likeable. He said he was a socialist, and, basically was saying the same things he is saying now. Mind you, this goes back many years, but Sherrod was right. You couldn't help but like the guy. His hair looked about the same back then, too.

Most of the interviews we did then were not to nail anyone to the wall. It wasn't about baiting them. It was just about giving them some time on the air and to enjoy their company. We'd do it from Sherrod's meeting room and we'd sit around the table and talk to each guest for about half an hour. Bernie was a lot of fun. We had him on twice when we went to D.C. Neither time did I see any intent to run for President. He was very popular in Vermont, but way out of the mainstream. I think maybe he thought things had changed enough, that maybe it was time. He put up a great fight.

We also had Hillary Clinton on a few times when she was a senator. One time we were in DeWine's office and I was talking to Jay Rockefeller across the table about some imminent shutdown that was going on. He was worried about that.

He was always a fun interview, and as he was leaving, the door behind me opened. I said goodbye to Jay and stood up and suddenly somebody came up behind me and tickled me. I turned around and it was Hillary Clinton.

She smiled and said, "Hi, I'm back." And it was like that every time she was with us. She was delightful, fun to have around, and likeable. There was nothing like the way some people describe her: domineering, evil and mean-spirited. She was delightful, loved to talk and we had a great time. Terrific personality.

I don't think we ever talked about her running for president. We never delved into anything that would have been detrimental to her or upset her. That was true with almost everybody who came on the show.

There were a couple times when there was something going on in Washington and the politicians didn't want to talk to the press at all, but they knew they could come on our show.

They knew they weren't going to be grilled. They were going to have fun, and it made them want to come in and do the show. Take Ted Kennedy, for example.

We always had fun with him. The first time I met him his dog was with him and it came up and stuck its nose in my crotch. Teddy made some wisecrack about it, like, "Maybe he knows you." I loved Teddy; he was great, and I liked to joke around with him. His dog was named Splash. So I would tell him, "I hate to say this but considering everything that's happened to you, especially Chappaquiddick, isn't that a bit insensitive of a name for a dog? Splash?"

"I know, I know; don't worry about it," he said.

Ted thought it was funny. He knew we had a great relationship and we would never talk about stuff like Chappaquiddick. We just talked about him and his life, and you had to realize how much responsibility he had with the whole Kennedy family looking at him to lead them on.

He tried to run for president and failed badly, but of all my political interviews, he was part of the one that was probably my most memorable.

One day I was sitting in Sherrod's office, talking on the phone to Elizabeth Edwards. It was 2008 and her husband, John, was running for president. She was in North Carolina, helping her folks move.

"This is amazing," I said. "You're in North Carolina helping your mom and dad move from where they are to someplace smaller, you're fighting cancer, which has gotten bad, and your husband's running for President, all at the same time."

"And don't forget: I've got a bunch of kids to take care of too," she replied.

"You know, you're amazing," I said. "You really are."

"Well, you just do what you gotta do. I'm going to fight this."

As I was talking to her, Teddy Kennedy walked into the room and could hear what was going on. So he came and sat down in the empty chair next to me. He put his hand up to his lips like "shhhh." And I stopped. Teddy said, "Elizabeth?" There was dead air for a minute. "Teddy?" she asked.

"Yeah, how are you?" he said. I'm not even sure that she knew him personally or not, but she recognized his voice immediately. He said, "I'm really proud of you and what you are trying to accomplish. I know what you must be going through."

Teddy said something that stayed with me. "I know a lot of people in this city. I know all the good doctors. I know all the medical people, and if there is anybody who I can get you in to see or anybody who I can help you with this whole thing that would make it better for you, all you have to do is ask and I'll see that it's done."

You could tell just how moved she was by that whole conversation.

We continued our conversation with Teddy, and when we were done he asked us to come up and visit him in Hyannis Port. "We'll do the show from there for a few days. That'd be fun, wouldn't it?" he said.

Gee, you think?

Sadly, that conversation with Teddy and Elizabeth was a forecast of things to come. By the time we returned to do the show the following year, we got a call from Teddy's office to tell us that he wasn't going to be there. He had just been diagnosed with cancer and had been taken by ambulance back to Hyannis Port. By the time we went back the next year, both Elizabeth and Teddy had passed on. It just makes you realize how temporary everything can be. You just never know when it's going to be over.

I hate to admit it, but my most boring interview was the result of a suggestion from Senator Dick Durbin of Illinois.

"I've got this guy you need to interview," Durbin said. "You're going to like him. He's going to be great. He's going places. He's going to be somebody." Dick had been on our show and he was really pushing for the other Senator from Illinois.

We took the WMJI morning show to Washington, D.C., once a year to interview politicians. Here I'm with Senator Hillary Clinton in the office of Senator Sherrod Brown, of Ohio.

Of course, it was Barack Obama.

So Obama came on and sat down. He was just there because Durbin had told him to do it. It was before he had decided to run for president. He was very guarded. He wasn't really laughing and having a good time. He was very serious and you couldn't really loosen him up at all. You really couldn't do anything with him.

We had Obama on twice in Washington and we had him back on the phone when he was running, but he was never fun. He was just a serious guy. Maybe he just didn't trust the media. From everything I've heard, his wife didn't trust the media at all. I don't know if he did or he didn't, but he was always very guarded. He was probably the worst interview of all of them.

Obama wasn't nasty and he wasn't mean. He just really didn't want to be there, and he was very low key with his answers. You couldn't get him to laugh or anything else. So remembering all the interviews with all the politicians, he was about the worst. He just really didn't respond.

I wasn't a fan of his at that point at all. I really didn't think he was going to make it into the White House, but Dick Durbin was right. He said, "This guy is going places." He was absolutely right.

So what do I know?

We were so successful taking our show to Washington, D.C. that eventually we took it even farther. Denny Sanders was our program director back then and he knew someone in London, so we took the show there three times. Then we even went to Hong Kong and Jerusalem.

In London we used these beautiful studios. They were on the top of the same building that Radio Free Europe had used. There was a glass partition between us and the British engineer. We'd been having a lot of theater people from New York who were doing shows in London come by.

But one day we were short on guests so the engineer asked us, "Would you like R2D2 to come by? He lives just down the block." We said "sure" and ten minutes later the guy shows up. *Star Wars* had just premiered so we talked about the movie. He said he had just stumbled into the role of R2D2. Now he was back in London doing local theater. When other actors came on the show, they were mobbed, but no one knew him out of costume.

We loved the actors! Theater and film. We had on lots of comics, too. One of them was a morning radio guy who was on the air in London and also did a show in Australia at the same time, which was pretty unusual. He sat in on the show and later came on the air with us in Cleveland. We had a different guest every half-hour. We also talked to some of the local London politicians, just like we did in Cleveland.

One of my favorite London memories had nothing to do with

the show. We were in the west end of London and my wife, Sandy, heard about this play. We didn't know anything about it, but it was *The Rocky Horror Show*. We were sitting there in the audience waiting for it to start when all of a sudden the guy who plays the transvestite came running down the aisle past us. We didn't have a clue what it was about. I'm a huge fan today; it's a mesmerizing play, but back then nobody knew what the play was about. We had no idea, but was an incredible evening.

Being a radio talk show host does have its perqs. Here's an example. In London we had a guy on who ran a big food awards program. We had learned a lot from him about the local restaurants, so we wanted to visit a little place behind the famous Harrod's department store. But when we went there they told us they were too busy for us, and we'd have to come back another time. So what can you do? I said "okay," but I also mentioned that we were from the States and were broadcasting nearby. Also that we had just had on the guy in charge of the London food awards program and that he had mentioned their place.

"You had the guy on from the London food awards on your show?" the host asked. "Why don't you go sit over there for a while and we'll see what we can do." About ten minutes later, he came back and seated us right by the window. Then he started interrogating us, "Did he tell you anything about the awards?"

Turned out, his restaurant was up for an award.

"No," I said, "he's not going to tell me if you won, but he did like you guys a lot and he said positive things about this place. That's why we came here."

"Good to know! Thank you so much."

We had a great meal, and he came back to talk to us a few more times, asking again about the awards show. Let's face it, it was the fact that the awards show guy was on our program that got us that table by the window.

It was Denny Sanders' idea to go to Hong Kong. He wanted to tie our visit in with the big ceremony going on when the Chinese would officially take their city back from the English. Chip Kullik went with me and we were probably the only radio show from the States there to see it. Hong Kong is a beautiful city. Before I went over I talked to George Wong from the Pearl of the Orient restaurant, who is a good friend. His family is from Hong Kong. So I tried to learn some of the language, like how to ask for a bathroom and how to say "please."

The top radio show in Hong Kong at the time was a duo, one English; the other, Chinese. We had the English-speaking guy on with us. We also had a lot of the local people on the show and even had a controversial preacher from Parma sit in with us. He was over there protesting something about the Chinese being oppressors.

No call-ins. We just had guests, people we found who were part of the whole takeover thing. We had a chance to talk to a lot of people over there, especially Americans. It was the end of an era and there were a lot of changes going on with the British giving up Hong Kong. They had a gigantic fireworks display that night, and Prince Charles sailed out of the harbor on his yacht to symbolize the turnover.

It was night when we finished our show because of the time change for mornings in Cleveland. We had to get back from the side of the island where the station was to the other side where our hotel was, but what a trip! There was a terrific crowd and traffic was a nightmare.

We found one cab that was open and we told the driver to get us back to our hotel. He was willing to brave the crowds and, since it was our last night there, we gave him one of our Majic t-shirts. There's a cabbie somewhere in Hong Kong driving around with a WMJI t-shirt.

It was raining when he dropped us off, but the fireworks display had just finished and the whole city was lit up. I'll always remember a Rolls Royce convertible pulling into the circle in front of the Peninsula Hotel where we were staying. The Rolls pulled up with the top down, in the rain, and there were two people in the front and three in the back, men and women, all dressed very elegantly. They were holding umbrellas up over their heads and bottles of champagne, drinking and partying.

They all piled out and the hotel guy said, "Go, go, go," and they ran inside. That will always be my vision of the Chinese taking back Hong Kong and the British leaving.

We were there for three days, and I remember one time in the hotel restaurant when the premier of China showed up. We were sitting in the lobby of the hotel and all of a sudden there were lots of cars pulling up to it. We didn't know what was going on, so we just walked into the restaurant and got a table. Then suddenly the elevator door opened up and the premier stepped out. He came out of the elevator, maybe twenty feet from us, and that was when we realized there was a red carpet on the ground from the elevator out to the door where they were going to take him away.

Everybody just stood there. The entire restaurant stopped. Then they all stood and applauded as he walked by. From everything I read later, it was very unusual for him to be in Hong Kong. I guess he usually stayed in the capital on the mainland, but he had been meeting upstairs with the people who were taking over the city and he was going to be visiting it more often. He had also pledged to pretty much leave it the way it was, a capitalist city in a communist country. None of us believed that would last, but it really has. It was really quite a thrill to see him walk by with his aides on the red carpet. That was certainly the high point for me in Hong Kong, being that close to a head of state.

Our trip to Jerusalem was probably the favorite trip of my lifetime. Our general manager, Jim Meltzer, was the guy who wanted to take us to Jerusalem since he was Jewish. Our studios were inside a newspaper facility and we'd do our show from there. It was an amazing experience.

We broadcast there for several days, and it wasn't just a leisurely vacation. It was a dangerous time back then, and everybody thought we were nuts. They would search your backpack for a bomb if you went into a restaurant. They had just had an explosion on a bus that had killed several people.

We still had a chance to really get to know the city while we were there. The folks we were with went out of their way to show us everything they could. One time a group of local doctors sat in on our show. They told us, "This is great. We used to listen to you all the time when we drove down Cedar Road to go to work." They were from the Cleveland Clinic and had relocated to Jerusalem's Hadassah Hospital. They told us about this amazing doctor who took care of all the nation's leaders, so we set up to do the show at the hospital. Not only that, we had a lady on with us who was very high up in the power rankings and she told us that the Prime Minister of Israel, Menachem Begin, had just been rushed to the floor above us. So we got a chance to talk to this famous doctor who was taking care of him, and I think Begin died just after that.

While we were there I wanted to visit the Jewish Holocaust Museum, so the people who were doing our show put it together for me. I told them I'd been to the Holocaust Museum in Washington and the one in Berlin, but I understood that this one was quite a venue and I wanted see it. They set it up for someone to meet me. I went by myself and there was a very attractive lady waiting for me.

"You're John Lanigan?" she asked. "I'm your guide."

"You know, you sure don't look like a guide," I said.

"I'm not. I'm one of the executives here, but I'm from Cleveland and I'm a fan. I used to listen to you. In fact, my husband is operating on someone today and he wanted to get away to take you around and show you the museum, but he couldn't."

Clevelanders show up everywhere!

Having a personal guide show me around the museum made it so much better because she gave me access to a lot of things that I don't think they show on tours: some incredible artifacts. I'll always remember her. We had a good two-hour tour and she told me about some of the other museums.

The next day they were going to take us to a school, but I wanted to go to Bethlehem instead. Now Bethlehem is in the middle of Jerusalem and is Palestinian. Jerusalem is, of course, Jewish. There is a wall around Bethlehem but we had our driver, Moshe, to help us. Best driver I ever had. He was assigned to take us around in this small Mercedes Benz and we went everywhere in it. I told him I wanted to see Bethlehem, and he told me, "Okay, but I can't go with you, you know."

"I understand," I said, "you're Jewish and they're Palestinian." Then he said one of his best friends is Palestinian and works in there.

"I'll call him and bring you up to the gate and drop you off there. You can go through and he'll meet you on the other side and take you through Jerusalem when you're done. I'll meet you there."

Sure enough, we went through the gate and there was this guy waiting to show us around. He took us to the grotto where Christ is said to have been born and the little church that you see on Christmas when people from all over the world are in Bethlehem. It's a small area and while we were there, we learned later, there was some police activity behind the wall in the courtyard.

Moshe said the police were there because a bunch of Palestinians were demanding jobs as policemen and they were holding the local cops at gunpoint. I commented that maybe the worst way to get a job as a policeman is to hold policemen hostage.

"Yeah, it was a bad idea and they arrested them," Moshe said. "They're in jail now, but that was right behind you while you were in there."

After we were done inside and saw everything that was important, the guide said, "We don't have much here. It's pretty quiet, and I kind of agreed to do this for nothing for Moshe. So would you mind coming to our gift shop?" Hey, why not? As we drove back, we found this wonderful gift shop that had anything you could think of. I bought some rosaries for my wife's family back in Colorado. If you're a Catholic, you can't get anything more important than a rosary from Bethlehem, so I bought several of those and a few other little things.

I happened to mention that I collect icons. I don't have many, but I'd bought a Russian one when I was in Helsinki and I had it sent back home. I've collected them over the years. They are these wonderful wooden paintings that were done many, many years ago. I asked the guide if they had any. They had a couple and nothing that I really wanted, but he said, "Let me show you something. You might be someone that I can actually show this to." He brought one out from the back room.

It showed a man being painted into an icon in front of the Virgin Mary. His severed hand was lying on the floor, bleeding. I'd never seen an icon like that.

"Let me tell you the story behind this icon," the man said. "This is a guy who kept painting himself into icons with his hands. He'd paint the Virgin Mary, but he'd always have his hands around her waist, like he was there. They told him to stop that, he couldn't do that. If you're going to paint the icon, paint it, but keep yourself out of it. Your hand can't be in there! But he did it again, so they took him and cut his hand off. That's what was depicted: the man standing with his hand on the floor bleeding out of his wrist and the Virgin Mary next to him. They cut off his hand!"

"Who did the painting?" I asked the guide. "The guy whose hand was cut off or somebody else?" He said it was hard to tell with an icon, but the victim might have been the artist. They don't really have the names of who did the icon paintings because they are on wood. You'll see them in churches in Italy and in Russian churches everywhere, large and small, But the story behind that one was just so amazing that I had to buy it.

"I'll take it right now," I said.

It was so unusual, and it wasn't cheap. I think it was $5,000, but you're not going to buy icons for much less than that. I had paid almost that much for the Russian one in Helsinki. So I bought it and took it back with me from Bethlehem to Jerusalem then carried it back with me to Cleveland. I still have it today above my fireplace mantel. It's just an amazing piece and still my favorite because it is just so bizarre. It's amazing that they cut his hand off because they told him to stop doing what he was doing, and he did it again.

When the guide took me back to the wall, we hugged and I thanked him, saying I hoped his business would get better. This guy had an incredible store and I felt I'd bought enough to pay for the tour and help him out. I went back and there was Moshe waiting for me on the other side of the wall.

We stayed at the big hotel in Jerusalem, the King David. It's one of the great hotels in the world. It was bombed in the 1930s but survived in great form. We'd sit in the bar and talk to the bartender and he would tell us these wonderful stories about all the famous people that he had served, from presidents to kings. They all stayed at the King David. He'd been there for thirty or forty years. It had been bombed and knocked down and built up again, and the bartender had survived to tell the tales.

I have a picture of myself with my hand on the Wailing Wall, putting a wish into a crevice, which is what you do. I really loved visiting Jerusalem and getting to see all those equally amazing people, like the doctors from the Clinic. Jerusalem is one of the most amazing cities I've ever been to in my life. I'm not overly religious. I was brought up a Catholic in Nebraska, but just to see it was great.

Before we left, Moshe drove us back into Tel Aviv and there was a small plane waiting for us. Chip Kullik and Jim Meltzer were waiting, so we flew over the Dead Sea, landed and got to see everything going on up the coastline. We saw the towns along the way that you hear about all the time on the news, and when we got back, Moshe was there again. He wanted to take us to different sites along the way, and the whole time we were there we never had a problem. There never was any kind of a threat. We never saw anything bad happen to anybody, and it was just a spectacular trip

Chapter Thirteen

The Lanigan Travel Agency

MOST OF MY RADIO audience isn't aware of it, but for a while I owned my own travel agency. My wife, Sandy, ran it for us. Here's how that all came about.

I was bitten by the travel bug when I worked in Denver the second time. One of our show's sponsors was a guy who owned a big electric company. We became friends and one day he asked me, "Would you like to go on a trip with us?" Sure, I said, I'd like to see more of the U.S. But he said, "No, we're going to Spain."

Spain?

"Yeah, we're going to Madrid. Would you like to join us? It'll be a fun trip."

Sounded good, but I had to get a passport. I did, and we went to Madrid. I have to admit it was a little weird. When we got off the plane it was the first time I'd ever seen so many guns. There were guards everywhere. Madrid had people hovering over you as soon as you came into the airport because there'd been some problems going on. This was back in 1969, so it shows how little the world has changed since then.

What a terrific time! We saw the greatest bullfighter in the world battle in a ring in Madrid. We shopped and visited the Prado

Museum where all the great art can be found. I didn't speak the language and I remember going into an ice cream store trying to buy a sundae. I had to try to explain to him the ingredients. I think by the time I finally got the sundae it cost something like $35 because each thing I asked for, he said, "Oh, okay." Even so, it was my first time overseas. I saw a gorgeous city and I definitely caught the travel bug.

Sometimes the station management would reward advertisers with a trip somewhere. They do that all over the country, or at least they used to. Once the radio station offered top clients a trip to the Greece and some of them wanted me to go along. I'm going to turn down a trip to Greece? We flew to Athens and had a great time. One morning we were staying at a hotel by the Acropolis and there was a march going on nearby. It was the communists, and they were marching in the streets. I noticed that they were waving some flags, so I thought it would be a fun thing to take one back home as a souvenir.

My excuse was that I was drinking some ouzo at the time. I decided to march in the parade to see if I could get a flag. I started talking to one of the girls who I was marching with and told her that I loved the flag she was carrying.

"Here, you take it," she said. "Carry it."

I started waving it around, but then one of our people came up to me and said, "John, if they get a picture of you marching in this parade with that flag and it shows up in Athens you'll be in a world of hurt. Get the hell out of there." I took his advice but I did get my flag. We toured Athens and saw some other Greek Islands. We didn't go on the air from there but it was work-related. It was more like a client party.

Sandy and I always wanted to go to Egypt, and it turned out to be one of our best trips ever. There's an interesting story how we became good friends with our tour guide. He was a Muslim and

Those are four poisonous snakes draped on my head and shoulders. My wife, Sandy, and I were visiting a snake cave on a vacation trip to Thailand. (The snakes were made docile with incense.)

a doctor, but he was working as a tour guide because he had to do a few years of service to his country before he could practice. I met him when I got off the plane. He walked up and said, "Do you need a guide? Someone to show you around?" He seemed okay, so he took us to the hotel and said he'd come back the next day, but he needed a couple hundred dollars to reserve him. I gave him the money and then when I got back to my room, I thought, *I am the dumbest tourist who ever lived. I gave him money and I didn't know how to find him!*

But sure enough, he showed up the next morning, ready to go.

He also took us to parts of Cairo that most tourists wouldn't see. One site was where one of the kings was buried, but the tourists went in one way and we went in the other. He showed us all kinds of wonderful things.

We had a chance to ride camels around the pyramids. Anything that was part of Cairo we got to see and it was because of him. We became very good friends. So when Sandy and I decided to fly down to Luxor on our own, he said he'd pick us up when we came back.

It was near the end of Ramadan, when the religious fasting was all over, and I said to him, "I'd like to take you and your girlfriend to dinner when we return." This is where culture shock sets in. He told me, "I don't know." They'd been going together for eight years and he said he'd never been alone with her. They always had to have family with them. The guide said, "They never let me go out on my own like that." Even so, he said he would ask. So when we came back to the airport and he picked us up he said, "I've got good news. They said I could do it. I can take her out to dinner, without them."

We all met at an outdoor restaurant. His girlfriend didn't speak any English but she loved to eat, and she ate like she hadn't eaten in months—Muslims fast during the day throughout Ramadan When we left Egypt he said he was going to come visit us. He got in touch a couple times and said he was working on going to the States and asked if we'd be there. We said, "Of course! Come see us," but it never happened.

On the way back our plane stopped in Rome. Right next to us on the runway was a plane that was just sitting there and the pilot was inside it. We looked out to see what was going on and it was a hijacking! Back then you ran into this stuff everywhere you went and this was a long time ago. Once again, it seems like nothing has changed, but it was actually worse then. If you remember that era, the 1970s, hijackings happened quite frequently, especially overseas. In this country they would hijack a plane and say, "Take me to Cuba." In Europe it was not uncommon to see planes being hijacked on a regular basis.

There was a lot of tension in the world. When we flew into Beirut on the way there, they told us, "Do not get out of your seat if you're not getting off the plane." We couldn't go inside the airport. We had to stay on the plane. We landed near the Red Sea and could see Beirut right there. It looked like Salt Lake City, with the mountains all around it. Just a beautiful city. Only about three or four people got off the plane and the plane sat in the runway with the stairs going up to it.

I was sitting in the first row so I got up and walked to the front near the stairs and looked down. The flight attendant asked, "What are you doing?" I explained to her that I just wanted to stand on the ground of Beirut and say I'd been there. She said okay, go ahead. I walked down and a guard with a gun ran up to me and asked, "What are you doing?"

I told him and he said, "You sound American." Sure am, and he said, "Me too!" He was from somewhere near Cleveland, a soldier stationed in Beirut in what was a military airport in many ways. So he said come on down and look around and he pointed out things in the background. I was still quite a way from the city but at least I got on the ground. I got a chance to see Beirut through a military guy who was stationed there at the time—and to top it off, he was from Northeast Ohio!

There were lots of problems in Beirut, even back then. The airport was closed about half the time because of bombs, and it's still going on today. A big one from ISIS just went off there as I write this.

Beirut at one time had to be one of the most beautiful cities in the world. The military guy said the nightlife was fun, the clubs and restaurants were great. It was a great place to live. Then it all went to hell with the battle between the two different Muslim sects, the Sunnis and the Shiites.

When we came back from Egypt, Sandy took a job at a travel agency, and since we liked traveling so much we bought it when the owner wanted to sell. We called it Lanigan's Northshore Travel Agency. Because we were travel agents, we could do something called "Famtrips." Fam was for "familiarization," and these were special trips for agents to familiarize themselves with an area of the world so you could send people there and talk to them about it. If you needed to know about somewhere there was a company that put you on these Famtrips. They were a great way to see these places. They had wonderful guides taking you around who really knew the area and who did it at a greatly reduced rate.

One of the great things about the travel agency was the people we came into contact with who were also working in the travel industry. We met these terrific tour guides but they did so many other things, like the Cairo guy who was a doctor. We met a guy in France who worked for the BBC, but also took people around.

We took trips all over the world thanks to that. We were able to visit England five or six times and France three times in one year, but one day Sandy came home and dropped a bombshell.

"Do you want to go to Siberia?"

Wait a minute. I thought travel there was restricted! She explained that they were just opening it up and we could visit there on a Famtrip and be among the first to see that side of Siberia. I think we were the second group to visit there from the States.

It didn't last long. They opened Siberia up for the tourists to come through there for a while, but within a year they changed their minds and decided to close it back off it again. So we were pretty lucky to have seen it when we did.

Siberia was quite an adventure. We went from Anchorage to a city on the east coast of that country. When we got there I discovered that they had lost my luggage, and I climbed up through the luggage chute to see if it was stuck in there. The tour guide said, "You're crazy! You can't do that over here!"

Maybe, but I need my luggage!

"They'll find it, they'll find it," he said. "Let's go to lunch and we'll see." Off we went and pretty soon they showed up and said they had my bags and they were in the hotel room. They were there when we arrived.

The idea was to take the Trans-Siberian railroad. It was pretty amazing. It was just like in the movie *Reds*. In the summertime it was filled with trees.

The train ride itself was interesting. We were in an upgraded section, compared to the Russians, who were traveling in the lower-class section. In one of the trains the air conditioning wasn't working. It was a hot Siberian summer and we had to push the windows down so we could get some air coming through, but it was great to travel on this historic train.

Along the way we stopped in Mongolia so the train could change engines. While we were there all these Mongolian people came out and stood next to the train with baskets full of food you could buy. Sandy said, "I'm not about to try that stuff. You'll get sick, and then you'll die." But I decided it was worth the risk. I had some Russian money, bought some food from the baskets and it was wonderful.

Siberia is so large that we went through seven time zones. It's massive. We finally made it to Irkutsk, which is on this incredible lake called Baikal, which I'd heard so much about. It's the deepest freshwater lake in the world. We took an airboat across the lake and there were some kids who had boxes of stuff they were trying to sell. They were mostly Russian t-shirts that you could buy to show you'd been there and all that. I bought a couple of them and took them back. I still have one of them.

Irkutsk was known as "The Paris of Siberia." It wasn't as big as Paris but it was a classy place on Lake Baikal. While in Irkutsk we visited this little restaurant that had a menu four pages long. But after reading it the waiter said, "This is all we have, this and this."

Two items, and one of them was the transparent fish. Sandy wouldn't eat it but I gave it a try. Even though it was cooked it was still transparent, a really strange dining experience.

The small village we visited was very quaint. It was like stepping back in time. Cows walked freely down the street, and we saw women walking with sticks across their shoulders with water buckets on both ends. They were carrying water back to their village homes from the beautiful river that runs through Irkutsk.

One day I was sitting on the dock looking at the river and there was a young boy painting on the dock. It was a picture of a wildcat face with hair coming out in all directions with a lot of colors and a great expression. I told him that it was really good. He spoke a little English, not much, and I'd learned some Russian by then, so I kind of asked him if he'd sell it. He said yes and while I don't remember what I paid for it, I've carried it with me for a long time. When I brought it back I had it framed and have had it ever since. It's still on the desk upstairs in my house.

After Siberia we visited Moscow, and I loved it. I thought it was an incredible city. I remember buying some clothes there and when I took out my American Express card, the lady said, "Ooh, platinum, very good, very good, that's great." The people liked to see us. The card, too.

As part of our Famtrip the tour guide showed us the subway system. Moscow's subway has these incredible stations that are beautifully decorated with chandeliers and everything. They really are spectacular.

We had ten people in our group in that subway and it was late in the evening. The subway was very busy with lots of people traveling in it and I was looking over the walls. I got kind of caught up looking at all the amazing artwork, and when I looked around everybody in my group was gone, including my wife. Nobody was there.

I walked around thinking "My god, they're gone!" Now I didn't know what the hell to do. I didn't want to get on the subway train because I didn't know where it was going and I don't read Russian. So I took the escalator back up to the top. I knew where they were going, that we were going to end up in Red Square in front of the Kremlin, by Lenin's tomb. That was supposed to be the last stop on the subway trip.

I took the escalator and found myself standing in a Russian neighborhood without a clue about where I was. I saw a cab and I flagged it down. I spoke no Russian so I said, "I want to go Red Square."

He looked at me like "I don't know what you're talking about." Luckily I was carrying a Russian-language book I'd picked up in New York. I took out the little book, opened it to Red Square and said, "Me, there!" I also held up a ten dollar bill and he said, "Oh, good."

I jumped in the back of a cab not knowing a damn thing about him or anything else. He just started driving and after about ten minutes he brought me to a street with an alley on the side and said, "Here, get out."

He pointed to the alley, which went up a hill, and gestured like "Go there." I remember thinking, "Okay, this could be the end of my life, but I'm going to go up that street anyway." When I got up to the top of the street, there was Red Square in front of me in all of its glory.

I wandered over to Lenin's tomb and looked at the Kremlin

Standing in front of Mount Kilimanjaro (I'm second from the left), just after climbing it.

and the great church that's also there, but still saw no sign of my group. Then suddenly I saw them coming from another direction. They came up to me and asked, "Where have you been?"

Huh? You people left me. I was lost! Even so, I had beaten them to Red Square on my own. I asked Sandy why she had left me and she said, "Hey, we had to get on the subway train. We didn't know where you were." She wasn't about to stay behind and get lost herself, but I wasn't happy. I yelled at the tour guide, "What the hell is the matter with you?" We kind of knew each other by then, and he said, "I knew you could take care of yourself. I wasn't worried about you." Maybe *he* wasn't worried . . .

That incident aside, we became quite good friends and I talked to him a lot on the trip. He was a Holocaust survivor. He had the numbers on his arm from being in Auschwitz. He had lived in Marrakesh outside Morocco for a time.

Despite the harsh memories, one of the places he took us to was Auschwitz. I had to ask him, "How can you take people in

there and walk through it after all those things were done to you?"
They had killed his entire family.

"It's just tourism, John," he said, "I don't care anymore. It
doesn't matter to me. It's just a job. I don't live there. I just go
back to Marrakesh." He showed me pictures of his beautiful home
there, but he took people from all over the world to Europe and
Russia because he knew it so well.

The flight back from Siberia to Anchorage on a Russian airline
was even more of an adventure than the flight there. Some of
the seats wouldn't lean back and others didn't have seat belts. A
couple of the passengers had animals on the seat with them, but
that's what I liked about traveling. You never knew what you were
going to experience.

There were a couple more trips that I took that weren't Famtrips, but they were still some pretty strange adventures.

One of the craziest was when I decided that I wanted to go
rafting on the best white water rapids in the world. I looked it up
and it was supposed to be on the Zambezi River below Victoria
Falls in Zimbabwe. We put it all together, found the right people
and went to Zimbabwe.

We started in Zambia and went across to Zimbabwe over a
big bridge between the two countries and spans Victoria Falls.
It's also the world's highest bungee jump. We thought, as long as
we're here, we ought to try it.

You stand on the edge of the bridge and they put a whole lot
of gear on you. Then somebody hits you on the shoulder and you
jump, diving out in the sky over the water below Victoria Falls.
You fall a long way and it happens so fast that you don't really
have time to think about it until you feel the rope start to pull you
back up. That's when you know you're not dead, you didn't crash,
the line didn't break, and you didn't hit the water. After the rope
pulls you back up, you bounce up and down a few times and you

come up higher each time. There are people under the bridge where the railings run along the side. They pull you back on to the bottom of the bridge, take you back up and get you out of there. It was an unbelievable experience.

After Victoria Falls we spent a couple nights before the white water rafting trip, which takes a week. We slept alongside the Zambezi River and the first day we started, I believe we hit 26 class-five rapids. That was the first day! Class five is about as tough as you want to do, because at class six it's dangerous and at class seven you take the raft out of the water and walk around the rapids. The first time we went it looked okay, but I was thinking about what would happen if I fell in. Then the next thing I knew, the raft took on one huge rapid and the whole boat turned up on its side.

I went into the water.

I thought to myself, *Okay, I'm not dead, I'm alive. I can come back up.* When I came up close to the top, I felt somebody grab my life jacket from behind and jerk me out of the water right back into the raft.

The guys in charge of taking us down the river were the same ones who had grabbed me. They had probably pulled a thousand people out of the water, and to be perfectly honest, after that first dumping, I kind of got used to it.

I don't remember falling out again but I'm sure I probably did. After that first time it felt like, *Okay, I can do this.* We hit some amazing rapids and at night we would pull the raft up and dock it along the bank. The really scary thing was that there were hippos all over the place on that river and you didn't want to mess with them. They are the most dangerous animals in Africa. They kill more people than any other animal, so you learn to stay far away from them. If you want a guaranteed way to die, get close to a baby hippo because the mom will send you to the Pearly Gates.

We were on the river for five days and as we went farther and farther down the rapids, they began to decrease in strength. By about the fourth day it wasn't bad at all, and on the fifth day we were back in Harare, the main city in Zimbabwe. It wasn't until later that we found out that we were visiting Zimbabwe during a very dangerous time. The U.S. Ambassador was a lawyer from Cleveland who had been on our radio show. He told us that the dictator there, Robert Mugabe, had been on his worst behavior while we were there. He was always a crazy man. Zimbabwe is a beautiful country, but we were warned that if you're flying out of there on the national airline, it was not unusual for Mugabe to just take the plane for his own use. Zimbabwe didn't have a private plane at his disposal. Luckily, nothing had happened. We flew out of there and got to the States with no trouble, but it sure was an interesting place to visit.

There was one last trip that stands out and I'm not really sure that I should talk about it, but I will. We visited Cuba when it was still forbidden. I was living in Florida at the time, and even though it was technically illegal to travel to Cuba, a lot of Americans still went there.

Tourists didn't go there because of the Trading with the Enemies Act. That meant there was nothing wrong with going there, but you couldn't spend any money. I had this friend and we took his boat from Ft. Lauderdale to Havana. We docked at the Hemingway Marina and the people in Cuba were very welcome and friendly. There were about a dozen other boats in the marina, all from the States. We slept there on the boat and didn't spend any money. We just wanted to see the country and then we left.

When we went through customs on the way back we told them what we had done. "We ate on the boat, we slept on the boat and we didn't bring anything to spend money on." Okay. Next?

I do have to confess that I did bring one thing across the border.

While we were there we visited their great rum factory. It was in a very nice part of town near their famous cigar factory.

The pope had been there just a few months before and I remembered reading about this special rum that he took back with him. I asked about it and they took me in the back of the factory and said they had another bottle. It was pretty expensive because it had aged like fifty years.

I bought it and I took it back with me on the boat. The whole time I was thinking, if we get stopped and the Coast Guard comes after us and we say we're just boating, they're going to ask, "Where'd you get this rum?" I'd have to throw the rum overboard before that happened and that was something I really didn't want to do. I just wanted to get it back home. Luckily, no one bothered us on the trip back.

We ended up at Marathon Key because of a storm and then had to drive back to Key West to go through customs. After we explained to them what had happened, they separated us to try to get us to admit we had spent money on this or that, but we all had the same story. I brought the rum back to share with my friends. Like they say, how sweet it is.

Chapter Fourteen

My Favorite Interview

OVER THE YEARS I interviewed thousands of guests on my radio programs. In fact, I still remember my first one, when I was working in Scottsbluff, Nebraska. I drove over to the University of Colorado in Fort Collins to interview Peter, Paul and Mary, the folk singers. After it was over I noticed that Mary had laid her cigarette pack down. So I asked her if I could have it.

"Sure, take it, kid; have a good time," she said. I told her that I didn't smoke but that I just wanted to keep it because it was hers. And I kept that souvenir for a long time.

Before I close this memoir I just have to mention the one interview that stands head and shoulders above the rest. It was my favorite interview because my guest was my son Jad.

It was 4 a.m. on July 20, 2012, and I was driving from my home in Bay Village to the WMJI studio in Independence, just like any other workday. As I drove I was listening to one of the national news stations. I do that a lot to keep up with what's going in the world for my show.

The big story that day was a shooting at a movie theater in Colorado. They said something like twenty people were dead. The theater was located in Aurora, a Denver suburb. *Oh, my god,* I thought. My son Jad was a police lieutenant there.

Then they named the theater and I realized it was almost right across the street from the police station. I'd just been there recently with my son for an awards ceremony. He had taken me there and I got to meet the chief and some of his co-workers. As I was driving they kept providing more details about the shooting, how many people were dead and how they had captured the guy who did it and were taking him away.

When I got to the station I called my son from the parking lot before I went up to the studio. I knew he'd probably be up even though it was five a.m. our time, which mean it would be three a.m. Rocky Mountain time. I had heard the shooting had happened around midnight.

He answered, and I said, "You're up, I guess."

"Oh yeah."

I asked if he was involved in the aftermath and he said, "Oh yeah, I am," but he also made it clear, "I don't want to talk about it at all."

Jad had wanted to go home and get some sleep. The incident had been going on for five hours or so.

"I don't want to bother you," I said. "You go ahead and wrap it up and get out of there." He went home and went to bed and I went to work. When I got off the air, the phone rang and it was Jad.

"I just thought I'd call you back," he said, "I didn't want to cut you off this morning but it wasn't a good time to talk about it." Then he told me the whole story. How the call had come in that there was a shooting in the theater across the street and there was a guy in there with a gun who was taking down people at random. He said he responded immediately because they were so close.

Since he was the lieutenant on duty, he was in charge of the cops going in there. Jad and his partner went in through the door first, and the shooter was still inside.

The shooter saw them and turned and headed for the back door. As Jad went down the aisle after him, his partner stayed behind to try to help the people who had been shot, many of them crying out, "Please, please help me." It was a gruesome scene. One of them was even holding in part of her stomach. His partner tried to help those he could, but Jad had to go past all those people asking him to do something and chase the gunman out the back of the theater.

Luckily, at that point other police officers were also coming around the outside of the theater. The guy's car was parked in the lot in the back so he was running to his car, maybe even to get more bullets. Jad chased him and the other cops coming around the side of the building got to him first.

They shouted out, "That's it; hand's up." He didn't try anything. He just gave up, and they arrested him. His name was James Holmes, and they took him away. As Jad was telling me the story it was breaking everywhere. It was the top story in the country, and he was explaining it all to me. I had to ask.

"Would you like to talk about it on my show?"

Jad wasn't sure he could but he went in that day and he talked to the chief, who said, "Okay, it's your dad, but this is the only one. I don't want any other interviews coming out about this. We have to put a lid on it."

The next morning we talked about the whole thing and it was really quite a touching interview. The people who listened told me later that they could hear the emotion going back and forth between us because he could have been shot. He could have been killed.

He described trying to help the people, but at the same time not knowing what to expect as he ran into that theater. Then he found out that it was just this one person, and he went after him and chased him out the back.

I ended saying, "Great to talk to you. I love you." Jad said, "I love you, too, Dad, but I've got to go back to work."

So we wrapped up the interview and responses poured in from everywhere, even Denver. A Denver TV news anchor, who'd been in Cleveland, called me and asked if he could do an interview with my son.

I told him I'd be glad to mention it but as far as I knew that's the only interview that's he was going to do. Sure enough, Jad replied, "No, we're not doing any more interviews. Period."

One of the local police departments, I think North Olmsted, wanted him to come and speak but he couldn't. President Obama invited him to the White House, along with fifteen or twenty other top police officers from around the country for a ceremony in the Rose Garden. Jad was one of the more prominent ones because of that shooting. I was really proud when he got that invitation, and then he called me for advice.

He said, "You've been there a lot. Where do I go?" I told Jad there's a restaurant in Georgetown that's one of my all-time favorites, called 1789. I told him, "That'll be a good place to go afterward." I made sure it was a memorable visit.

He'd never been to Georgetown so I called the restaurant and I talked to the owner. I told him Jad was coming and the story behind it all. They made a reservation for him and I asked if he could have a bottle of Silver Oaks wine sitting on the table when he arrived, a wine we both like. The staff greeted him when he came in with his wife. The bottle of wine was sitting there and it made him feel really special. The bottom line is that he got a great evening out of it and he got to tour D.C. before he flew back to Denver.

Eventually the chief lifted the lid on interviews. Since then he's been invited to speak all over the world, even Hawaii and Tibet. That's right, Lhasa, Tibet! He spoke to the police and they took him around the city and showed him the landmarks, like where the Dalai Lama lives. Jad's spoken to Cleveland-area police departments and all over the country. They all want to ask him how to handle something like that if it happens in their towns. It's become a large part of his career.

Jad was by far my favorite guest. We still talk about it a little bit but I don't get into it too much with him. I think he's happy. He lives really well but I'm sure he has lots of memories to deal with in his sleep. But he seems to be doing okay.

I've always felt very lucky to have two great kids—Jad, the police lieutenant, and my older son, Jeff, who is a paramedic and chief of the Parker, Colorado, Fire Department. They both risk their lives and do dangerous things. I have no idea where they got that from.

Chapter Fifteen

Johnny's Back!—"The Spew"

A GOOD PERFORMER KNOWS TO leave when he's on top. I've accomplished more than I had ever imagined, and when I retired from WMJI in 2014, I thought I was retired for good. I didn't want to do radio anymore at all. I was planning to move to Florida and lead the good life.

But then I came back to Cleveland in the summer of 2015 and Keith Abrams, the operations manager for iHeartRadio, asked me to meet him for dinner. iHeartRadio used to be Clear Channel and owns seven channels in the same building in Independence. WMJI, WTAM, WGAR and the others each have their own program directors, but Keith is the boss of them all.

Abrams asked if I had any plans.

"Not really," I said. "I'm done and I live in Florida anyway so I can't do anything."

"Okay, but think about his. *The Spew* is on from 9 to 10 every morning with Mike Trivisonno and Bob Frantz, but Bob is leaving and we haven't found anybody to replace him. We thought it would be fun if you came back and tried it until we found somebody. It would give you something to do for a little while and see how it works."

The Spew was kind of a debate show where Triv and Frantz would debate the trending topics of the day for an hour each morning. I thought about it, but I wasn't too hot about working with Trivisonno because he used to make fun of me on his show when we were competing against each other. I just put up with him the whole time.

I had never met him even though his office was just around the corner from Majic's studio in Independence, probably because I worked mornings and he worked afternoons. I'd seen him a couple times but never spoke to him. When he made fun of me at different times, I just ignored him. But the powers that be figured it might be interesting "confrontational radio."

"Why not?" I said. "I'll try it. What the heck."

A year later, Gary Mincer, our general manager, told me that he couldn't believe it was still on the air.

"After they asked you to do it," he admitted, "I really didn't think it would last for more than three days before you told Triv to go to hell and left."

In the beginning Triv worked from his home and I came into the studio. Then Triv actually started coming in also and we did it live in the studio. We were sort of feeling our way around to see how it would work. One day he said, "Let's just do the show with me interviewing you.

"Fine," I said, "as long as I can interview you the same way tomorrow."

We started making fun of each other, got to know each other and it went on from there. Everybody said it was really working and the ratings got better. We kept doing it until the end of the summer when it came time for me to go back to Florida and I told them I couldn't do it anymore. I didn't make any plans to stay. I was still leaving.

The management had another idea: How about if they put a

line into my house in Florida? They'd come out and install the line and I'd be directly connected to WTAM. I could do the show from there. Some folks from the Florida station WFLA helped me hook it up, and they were great. The engineer who came over my house was my old engineer from when I worked in Tampa. We got everything in and it worked for a while, but it had some bugs in it. It would just cut off, and there were times when the phone company just disconnected the line for some reason. Other times the connection was just terrible.

Eventually I said I didn't want to do it anymore because it was really not working. They came up with another idea.

"How about if we give you a Comrex unit?" they said. I didn't know a Comrex unit from a bubble gum factory. "All you have to do is plug it in in the morning and turn it on and you'll be with us live in the studio."

"From anywhere?" I asked.

"From anywhere."

The Comrex was about the size of a hardcover book. The WFLA engineers came over again and showed me how to use it. Now I can sit out on the patio in my back yard and do the show from a table by the pool. I just plug it in, hit two buttons, and up comes WTAM.

I've been doing it that way ever since.

Every afternoon, the program director, Ray Davis, sends out ten questions that are going to be the topics for the show the next day and we just go through the list. We fight back and forth and that's how we do *The Spew*. It's really easy. We don't have guests, although they do take phone calls sometimes. Our host and moderator, Mike Snyder, does a great job. He has control of everything in the studio. When I come back to Cleveland I'll just go in and do the show live. That way I don't have to bring the Comrex unit with me.

Basically, I just go back and forth with Triv. We don't agree much on anything, but it seems to work. As Davis saw it, "I think it works because you guys don't have anything in common. You pretty much make fun of him and he makes fun of you. He has his own ideas and you have yours. Yet you seem to get along off the air." And, yeah, we do.

The way it sounds on the mic is not quite the way it is off the air. We each have a part to play, even though sometimes it does get a bit too personal. Sometimes it'll get really heated, like when he would get carried away about Trump and I made fun of him. Trust me, the folks who listen out there have plenty of opinions, too. They'll text or email comments like, "You're an idiot. You don't know what you're talking about." I read some of them and think, "Okay, this isn't brain surgery. Why are these people getting this upset about things? I'm just not going to let it get to me that much." It's not always easy, but that's *The Spew* and why people like it. I don't know if I'll still be doing it when you read this, but it was fun while it lasted.

People ask me what I see for the future of radio. The Internet is the future. Like FM, people will tune in to Internet radio when it's in their cars. That's coming. I listen to Sirius when I'm in the mountains. Jimmy Buffet's *Margaritaville*. Five or six other channels. It's a bit like Internet radio will be.

And my own future with radio? When it's over at WTAM, I really am going to retire. I'll sit back, enjoy our places in Florida and Colorado, spend time with my family, and maybe tell my grandchildren stories that they may or may not believe about how their grandfather once made a living.

About the Co-Authors

PETER JEDICK is the author of four books, including *The West Tech Terrorist* and *Hippies*. He has written for several national magazines, including *America in World War II* and *Baseball America*, as well as for the *Plain Dealer, Cleveland Magazine*, and Sun Newspapers. He received an Excellence in Journalism award from the Press Club of Cleveland and has appeared as a radio commentator on WKSU-FM.

MIKE OLSZEWSKI is an award-winning radio and TV journalist who now teaches courses on media and popular culture at the university level. He documents Cleveland's media history, along with his wife and co-author, Janice Olszewski, in books such as *Cleveland Radio Tales, Cleveland TV Tales*, and *Radio Daze*.

OTHER BOOKS OF INTEREST . . .

Cleveland Radio Tales
Stories from the Local Radio Scene of the 1960s, '70s, '80s, and '90s

Mike Olszewski, Janice Olszewski

Meet some of the most eccentric personalities in Cleveland radio history! These tales, from the 1960s to 1990s, share on-air and off-air antics of radio hosts who performed in the nude, battled station owners (and sometimes brawled with each other), broke major news stories, discovered new musical acts, and tried any stunt to grab listeners' attention.

The Buzzard
Inside the Glory Days of WMMS and Cleveland Rock Radio—A Memoir

John Gorman, Tom Feran

This rock and roll radio memoir goes behind the scenes at the nation's hottest station during FM's heyday, from 1973 to 1986. It was a wild and creative time. John Gorman and a small band of true believers remade rock radio while Cleveland staked its claim as the "Rock and Roll Capital." Filled with juicy insider details.

"Gorman describes in exclusive, behind-the-scenes detail the state of rock 'n' roll from the early '70s to the late '80s, when just about anything happened and everyone looked the other way . . . Essential reading for musicians, entertainment industry leaders, and music fans." – Mike Shea, CEO/Co-Founder, Alternative Press magazine

Cleveland TV Tales
Stories from the Golden Age of Local Television

Mike Olszewski, Janice Olszewski

Remember when TV was just three channels and the biggest celebrities in Cleveland were a movie host named Ghoulardi, an elf named Barnaby, and a newscaster named Dorothy Fuldheim? Revisit the early days in these lively stories about the pioneering entertainers who invented television programming before our very eyes. Filled with fun details.

Read samples at **www.grayco.com**

OTHER BOOKS OF INTEREST . . .

Cleveland Rock and Roll Memories

True and Tall Tales of the Glory Days, Told by Musicians, DJs, Promoters, and Fans Who Made the Scene in the '60s, '70s, and '80s

Carlo Wolff

Clevelanders who grew up with Rock and Roll in the 1960s, '70s, and '80s remember a golden age, with clubs like the Agora, trendsetting radio stations WIXY 1260 and WMMS, Coffee Break Concerts, The World Series of Rock. Includes first-person stories by fans, musicians, DJs, reporters, club owners, and more, with rare photos and memorabilia.

Cleveland TV Tales Volume 2

More Stories from the Golden Age of Local Television

Mike Olszewski, Janice Olszewski

More behind-the-screen stories from Cleveland TV history (1960s-'90s), including the rise of glamorous news anchors with big hair and perky noses, battling horror-movie hosts, investigative reporters stalking wrongdoers on both sides of the law, a daytime host's bizarre scandal, a mayor who co-hosted with a ventriloquist's dummy, and much more.

Big Chuck!

My Favorite Stories from 47 Years on Cleveland TV

Chuck Schodowski, Tom Feran

A beloved Cleveland TV legend tells funny and surprising stories from a lifetime in television. "Big Chuck" collaborated with Ernie Anderson on the groundbreaking "Ghoulardi" show and continued to host a late-night show across four decades—the longest such run in TV history. Packed with behind-the-scenes details about TV and celebrities.

"A vivid picture of an honest man in the insane world of television. Highly recommended." – Midwest Book Review

Read samples at **www.grayco.com**